T0061013

ESSENTIAL CONCEPTS

KEYBOARD Voicings

THE COMPLETE GUIDE

by Kevin King

ISBN 0-7935-8204-0

HAL•LEONARD®
CORPORATION

7777 W. BLUEMOUND RD. P.O. BOX 13819 MILWAUKEE, WI 53213

Visit Hal Leonard Online at
www.halleonard.com

Table of Contents

Intervals

1

n order for a musical event to be described as a chord, it must contain at least two notes, played simultaneously. The distance between these two notes is known as an *interval*. For example, on a keyboard, the interval from white key to black key is called a *minor 2nd*.

This interval is also referred to as a *half step*, which is the smallest interval we will encounter in chord construction. You can locate any larger interval by simply counting up or down the keyboard in half steps.

minor 2nd

minor 2nd or "half step"

Here is a table you can use as reference:

half steps	interval name
1	minor 2nd
2	major 2nd
3	minor 3rd
4	major 3rd
5	perfect 4th
6	tritone
7	perfect 5th
8	minor 6th
9	major 6th
10	minor 7th
11	major 7th
12	octave

Note: *Once you begin to locate and play these intervals, it will not be necessary to use this half-step method, but in the meantime it should come in handy!*

Chord Symbols

Throughout this book, we will use letters and numbers together to form symbols that tell us what chord to construct. These are known as *chord symbols*.

In upcoming exercises, both the notes on the staff and the chord symbol will be used. But in today's music, in many instances, only the chord symbol will be present. So, be sure that you associate the chord shapes you are learning with the chord symbol being used. Here are a few examples of common chord symbols.

The Power Chord

The first interval we must become familiar with if we are to construct chords is the *perfect 5th*. As you can see from the table on the previous page, a perfect 5th consists of two notes, seven half steps apart. When played together, this interval creates the shell of a basic chord. This shell is also known as a *power chord*.

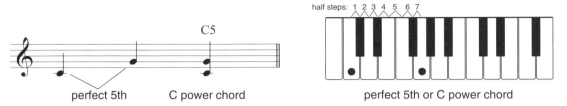

The power chord is given a chord symbol that represents the letter name of the "root" (the lower tone in this example) and the number 5 to indicate the perfect 5th interval.

Exercise 1: Locating and Playing the Power Chord

Play the following drill with both hands.

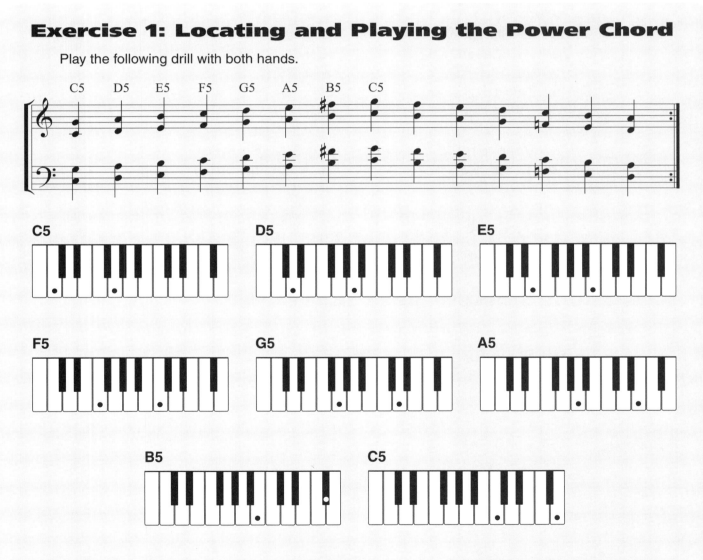

Note: While practicing this exercise, pay close attention to each pair of notes you play. Work on attaining both the physical feel and mental picture of these intervals. This will be very important as we begin to build larger chords.

Inversions

An *inversion* is the rearranging of chord tones. This is the essence of chord *voicing* (the order and register in which we play chord tones from bottom to top). Since the power chord only contains two notes, there are only two possible arrangements:

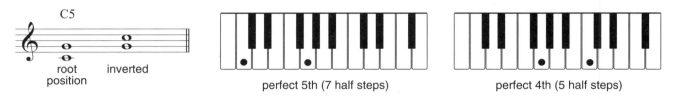

perfect 5th (7 half steps)   perfect 4th (5 half steps)

It is important to have a clear understanding of intervals and their inversions. Here is a table showing simple intervals and their inversions:

interval		inversion
minor 2nd (1 half step)	⟶	*major 7th* (11 half steps)
major 2nd (2 half steps)	⟶	*minor 7th* (10 half steps)
minor 3rd (3 half steps)	⟶	*major 6th* (9 half steps)
major 3rd (4 half steps)	⟶	*minor 6th* (8 half steps)
perfect 4th (5 half steps)	⟶	*perfect 5th* (7 half steps)
augmented 4th (6 half steps)	⟶	*diminished 5th* (6 half steps)
perfect 5th (7 half steps)	⟶	*perfect 4th* (5 half steps)
minor 6th (8 half steps)	⟶	*major 3rd* (4 half steps)
major 6th (9 half steps)	⟶	*minor 3rd* (3 half steps)
minor 7th (10 half steps)	⟶	*major 2nd* (2 half steps)
major 7th (11 half steps)	⟶	*minor 2nd* (1 half step)

Up to this point, we have only explored the perfect 5th, which you now know inverts to a perfect 4th. We will discuss other intervals and inversions in upcoming chapters. Use the following exercise to get a physical and mental "feel" for the perfect 4th interval.

Exercise 2: Power Chord Inversions

Play the following drill with both hands, in tempo:

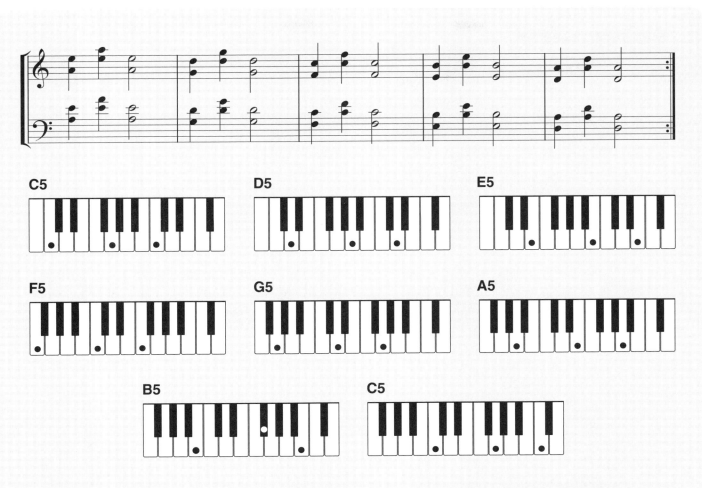

Note: *As you may have noticed, we have only built power chords on the white notes of the keyboard. Once you are comfortable with those, locate and play power chords built on the black keys:*

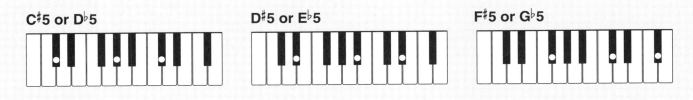

Once you have mastered Exercises 1 and 2, try choosing power chords and their inversions at random or in a progression:

Also, see if you can do the same exercise beginning with the perfect 4th interval:

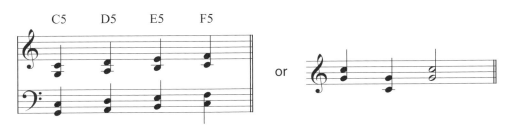

This should help to strengthen your on-sight recognition of these two-note chords.

Summary

1. The distance between two notes is called an _____.

2. A perfect 5th is made up of _____ half steps.

3. Two or more notes played simultaneously is called a _____.

4. The "power chord" is comprised of how many notes? _____.

5. When chord tones are rearranged, it is called an _____.

6. What interval is an inverted perfect 5th? _____.

7. Which chord symbol in this chapter contained a black key? _____.

Remember: You must master the previous exercises in order to be prepared for upcoming chord information. All the information and drills in Chapter 1 will become invaluable as you proceed through this book. Also, the ability to perform all drills in tempo will build good eye-to-hand coordination for future studies.

The Triad

A *triad* is a three-note chord containing the 1st (root), 3rd, and 5th scale steps of the coinciding scale. For example, a C major triad, contains the *natural* 1st (root), 3rd, and 5th scale degrees of a C major scale:

As you can see, we have simply added a third note to our power chord to create the triad. This new note, the *major* 3rd, is four half steps above the root.

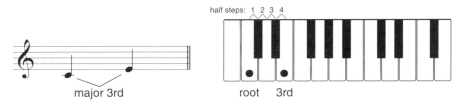

Once the 3rd is added, the chord takes on a "quality." The 3rd of the chord defines that quality; therefore a *major* 3rd will create a *major* chord quality.

The chord symbol for a major triad is simply the letter name of the root with no suffix added:

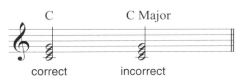

Here are all twelve major triads in root position:

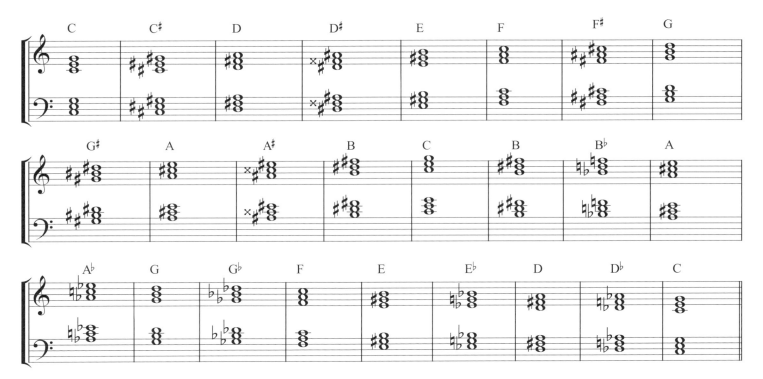

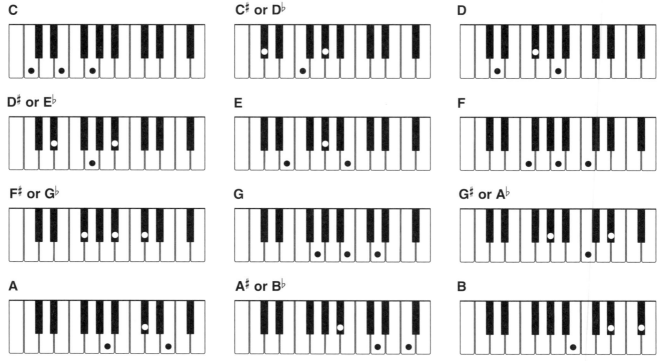

Exercise: Chromatic Triads

Locate and play all root position major triads by first arpeggiating the chord tones separately, immediately followed by the entire triad. Play the exercise with both hands, in tempo. Keep practicing this until it can be performed without hesitation.

Refer back to the illustrations above if necessary. As you practice this exercise, begin to internalize the sound of the major "quality." Again, attempt to get a feel for this shape as well as a mental picture of the note groupings.

Inversions

3

n Chapter 2, you practiced triads in *root position*. This means that the chords were voiced with the root as the lowest tone. If a chord tone other than the root is used, the chord is said to be *inverted.* Because there are only three notes in a triad, there are only three possible inversions:

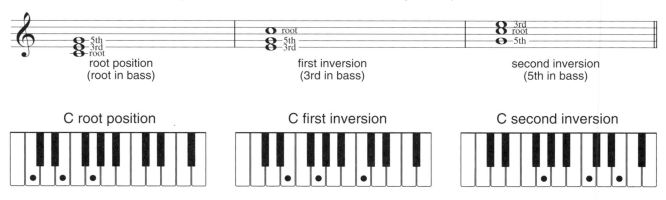

| root position (root in bass) | first inversion (3rd in bass) | second inversion (5th in bass) |

C root position   C first inversion   C second inversion

As you can see from the illustration above, first and second inversions incorporate the use of the perfect 4th interval, as seen in the power chord from Chapter 1. Since the root position voicing involves only intervals of a 3rd, the ability to see and "feel" this larger interval will help recognition, speed, and accuracy. Memorize these three-note groupings by their individual letter names and corresponding scale degrees. Later, as our chords become more complex, this will prove to be an invaluable skill.

Here are all twelve major triads and their inversions:

C   root position   first inversion   second inversion

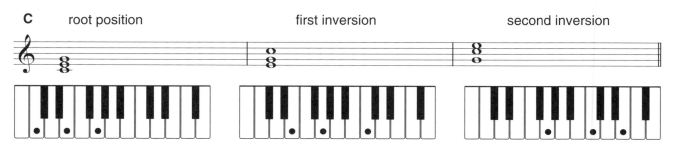

C♯ or D♭

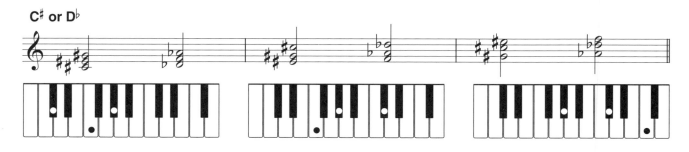

D

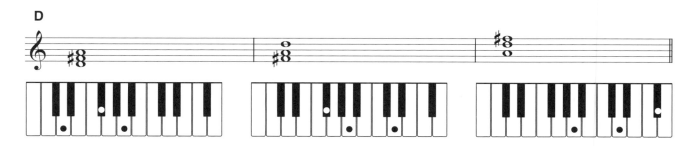

D♯ or E♭

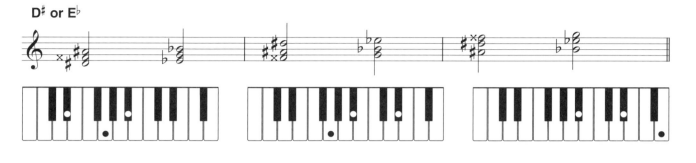

E

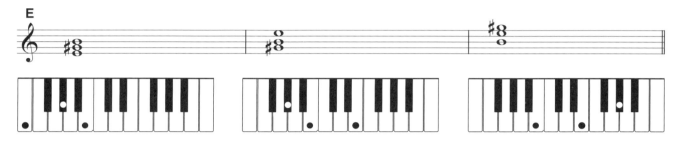

F

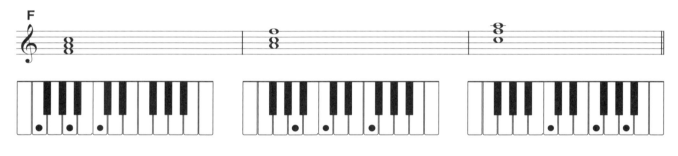

F♯ or G♭

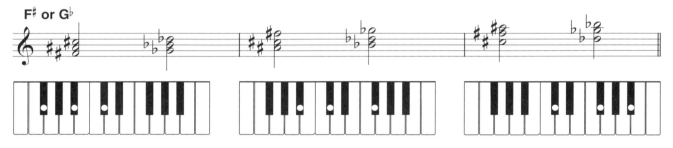

G

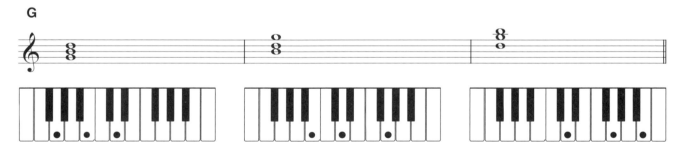

G♯ or A♭

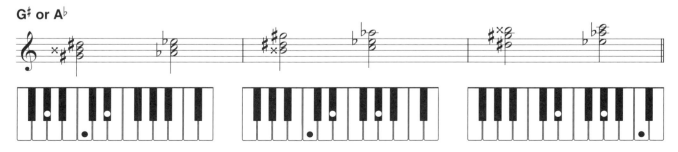

A

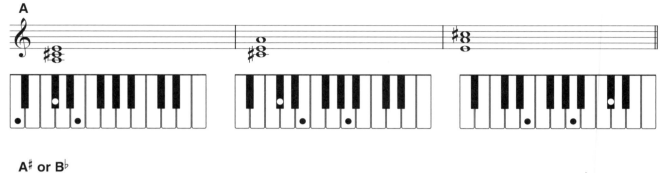

A♯ or B♭

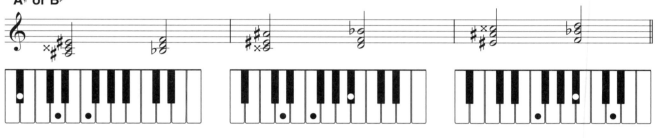

B

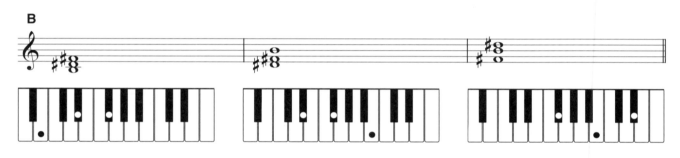

Exercise 1: Chromatic Triad Inversions

The next two exercises will help build major triad recognition and performance through a strong rhythmic regimen. *It is crucial that you master these drills!*

Practice the following exercise until is can be performed without hesitation.

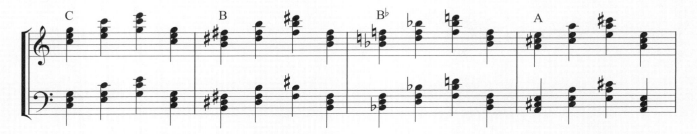

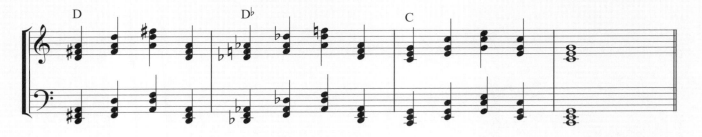

3

Exercise 2: The Inversion Polka

This next exercise moves through triad inversions in a cycle of 4ths. The left-hand part creates a bass line while the right hand answers with the chord. Practice the following exercise until it can be performed without hesitation.

Voice Leading

4

When moving from chord to chord (as in a chord progression), if the same inversion is used repeatedly, abrupt movement is inevitable. In order to "smooth out" this movement, we must use alternating inversion. This technique is called *voice leading*. The principle behind this technique is to use the inversion closest to the chord just played. This is done by keeping any *common tones* in place. In some cases, only the bass note will need to move. In turn, there will be times in which no tones are common, so all pitches will move. See the example below:

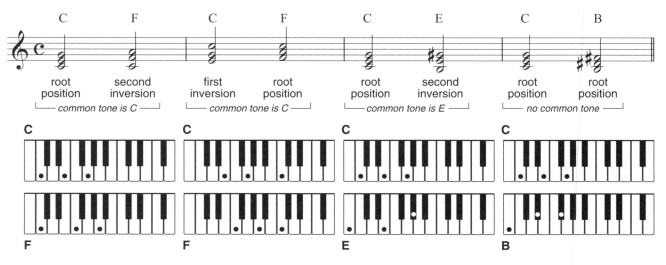

As you can see and hear, voice leading creates the smoothest possible transitions. This technique becomes even more valuable when larger and more complex chords are introduced. Hopefully, you are now understanding the importance of the preceding exercises. If a strong mental and physical foundation in inversions is not obtained, the use of voice leading becomes very difficult.

Exercise: Voice Leading I to IV

Practice the following exercise until it can be performed without hesitation. Be sure to perform the triads in their written register.

Chapter 4

The Minor Triad

5

The other chord quality that creates harmonic stability is the *minor* triad. It is similar in shape and feel to the major triad in that its shell (root and 5th) is the same. The difference is that the 3rd, which defines the chord's quality, is a *minor* 3rd (three half steps) above the root. To find the minor 3rd of a triad, count up three half steps from the root, or simply lower the 3rd of the major triad 1/2 step.

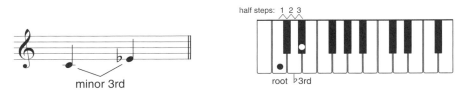

A minor triad is a three-note chord containing the 1st (root), 3rd, and 5th scale steps of the *natural minor scale.* For example, C minor contains the *natural* 1st (root), 3rd, and 5th scale degrees of a C minor scale:

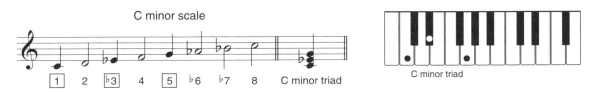

The chord symbol for a minor triad is simply the letter name of the root with the suffix "mi" added:

Here are all twelve minor triads in root position:

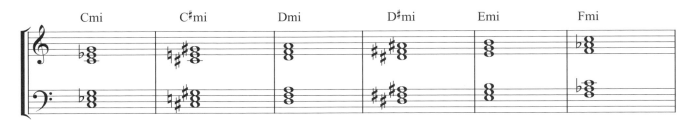

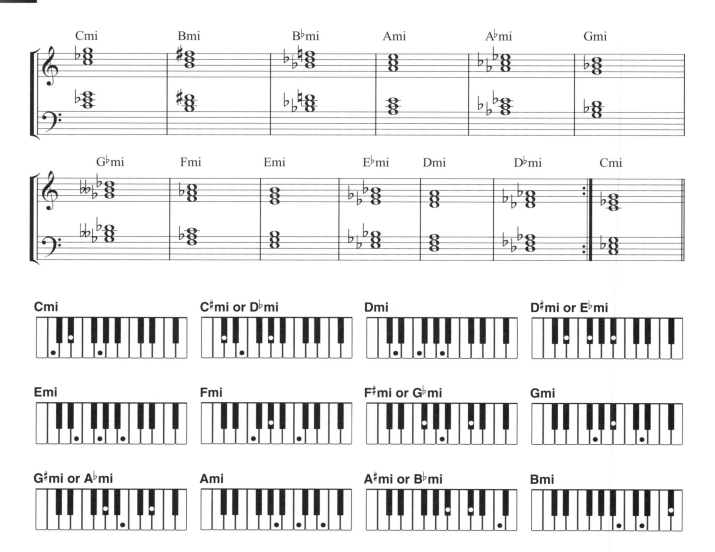

Exercise 1: Chromatic Minor Triads

Locate and play all root position minor triads by first arpeggiating the chord tones separately, immediately followed by the entire triad. Play the exercise with both hands, in tempo. Keep practicing this until it can be performed without hesitation.

Refer to the illustrations above if necessary. As you practice this exercise, begin to internalize the sound of the minor "quality." Again, attempt to get a feel for this shape as well as a mental picture of the note groupings.

Chapter 5

Minor Triad Inversions

Here are all twelve minor triads and their inversions:

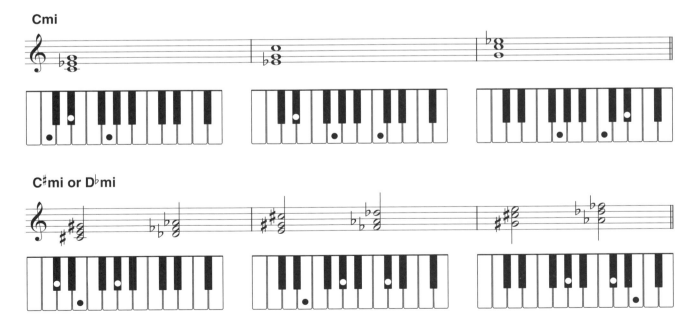

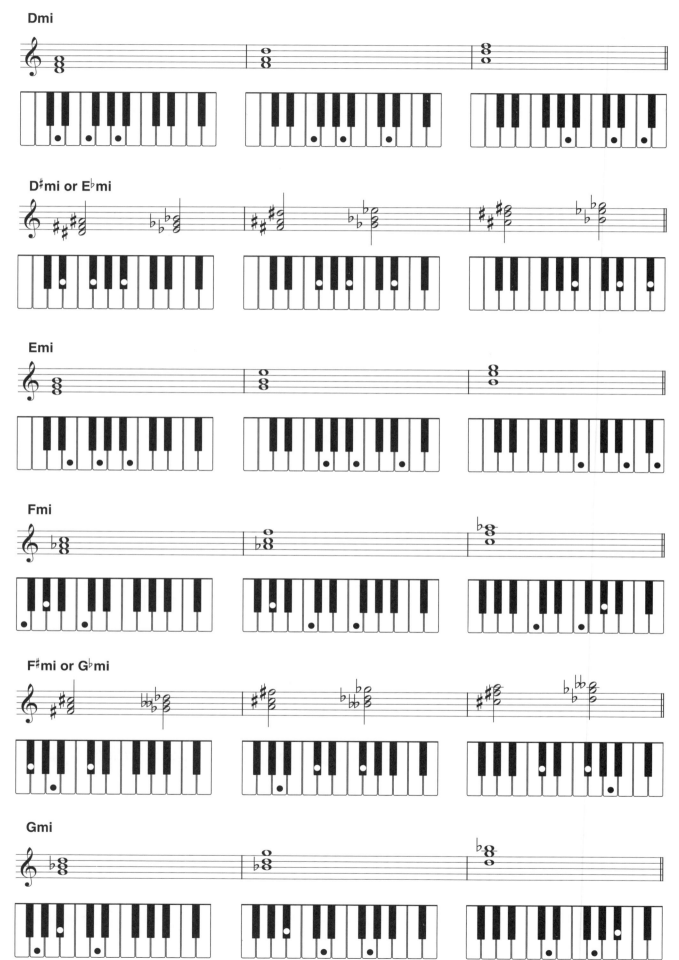

G♯mi or A♭mi

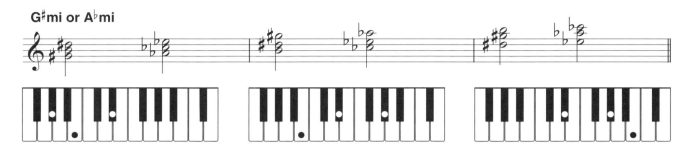

Ami

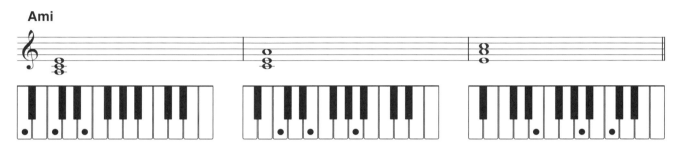

A♯mi or B♭mi

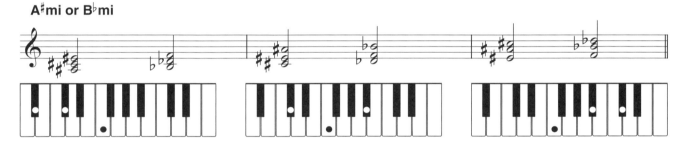

Bmi

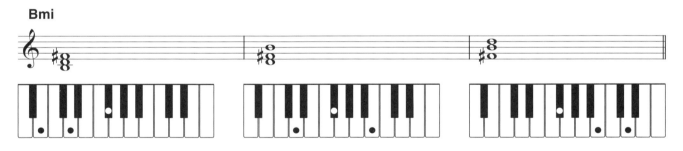

Exercise 2: Chromatic Minor Triad Inversions

This exercise will help build minor triad recognition and performance through a strong rhythmic regimen. *It is crucial that you master this drill!*

Practice the following exercise until it can be performed without hesitation.

The Diminished Triad

6

The chord quality we will discuss in this chapter is quite different from major and minor. First of all, it does not evoke a feeling of stability. Instead, the *diminished* chord quality creates musical tension, or instability. In essence, this type of chord will always feel as if it needs to *resolve*. Also, the diminished triad does not use the same "shell." Because of this, diminished triads have a slightly different shape and feel on the keyboard. The difference is that the 5th is a diminished 5th (six half steps) above the root. To find the 5th of a diminished triad, count up six half steps from the root, or simply lower the 5th of the minor triad 1/2 step.

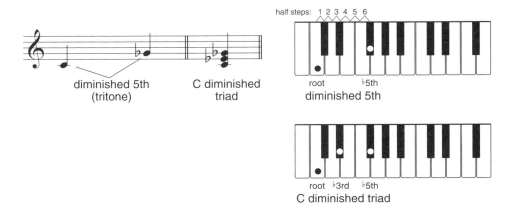

Note: *The interval of a diminished 5th is also referred to as a tritone.*

It is important to note that both the major and minor scale have this tritone interval in their construction:

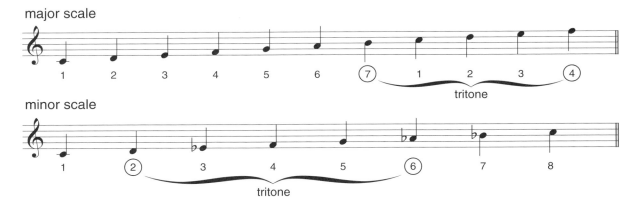

The chord symbol for diminished is the letter name of the root followed by the symbol "o":

Here are all twelve diminished triads in root position:

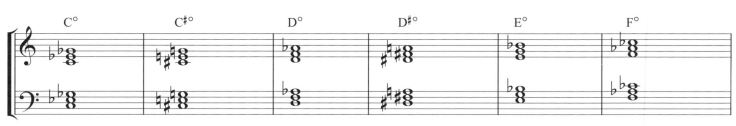

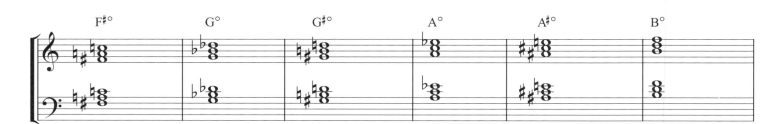

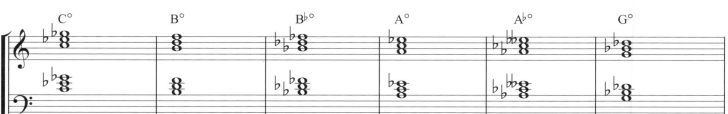

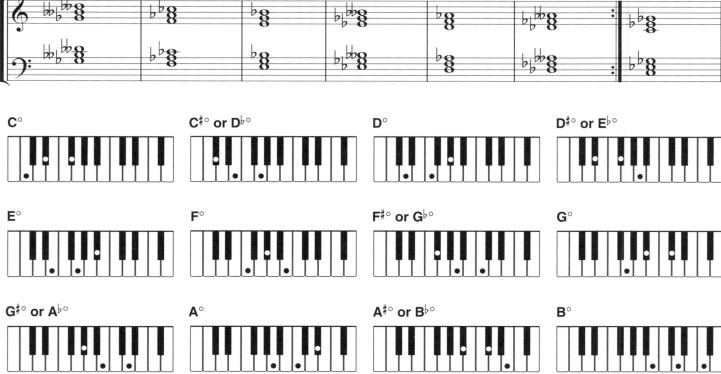

Exercise 1: Chromatic Diminished Triads

Locate and play all root position diminished triads by first arpeggiating the chord tones separately, immediately followed by the entire triad. Play the exercise with both hands, in tempo. Keep practicing this until it can be performed without hesitation.

Refer back to the illustrations on the previous page if necessary. As you practice this exercise, begin to internalize the sound of the diminished "quality." Again, attempt to get a feel for this shape as well as a mental picture of the note groupings.

Diminished Triad Inversions

Here are all twelve diminished triads and their inversions:

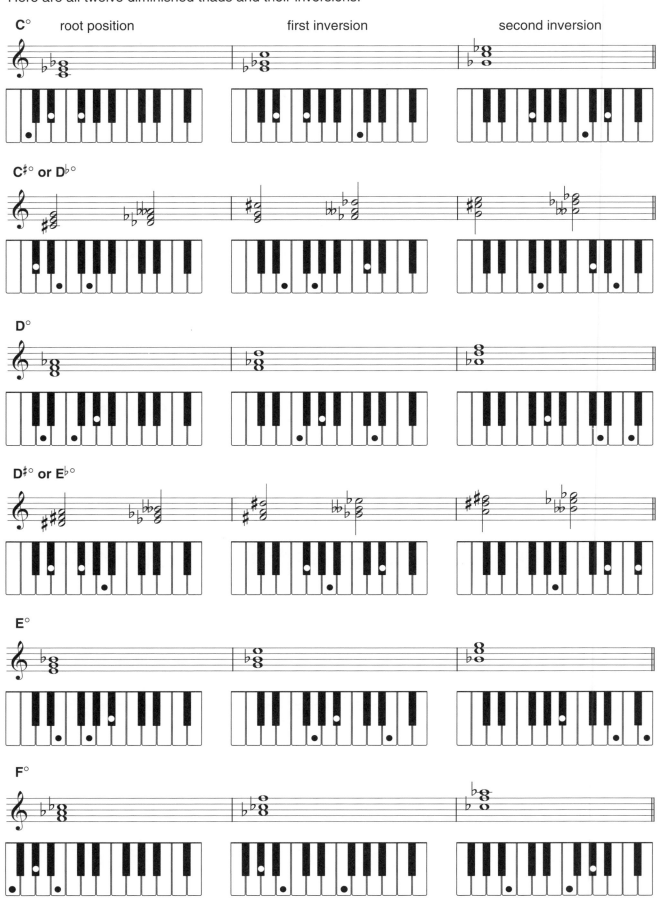

F#° or G♭°

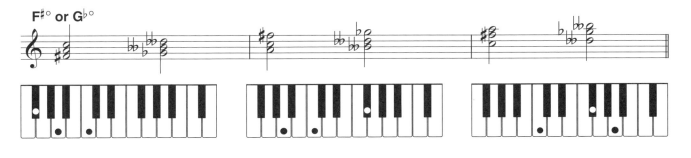

G°

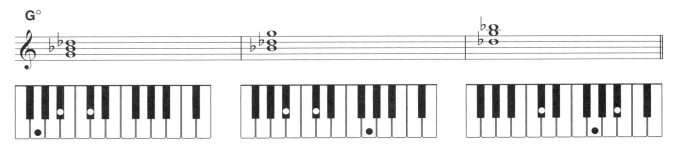

G#° or A♭°

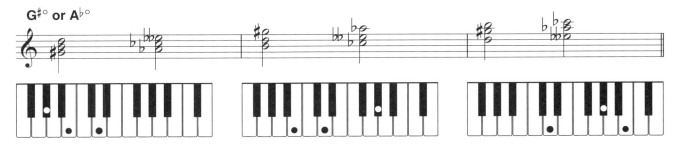

A°

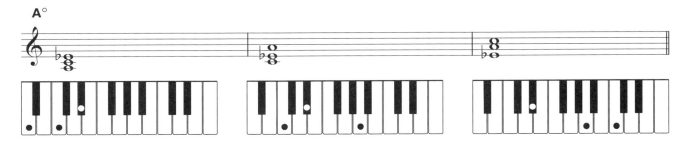

A#° or B♭°

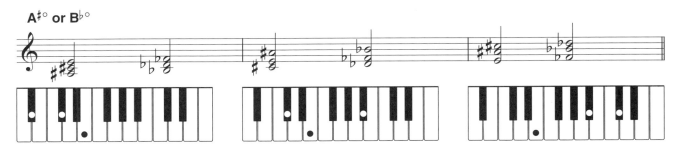

B°

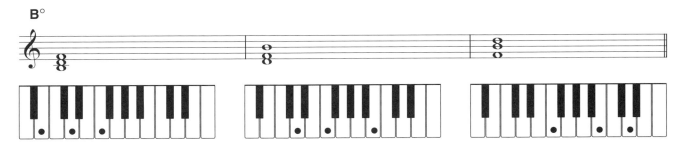

Exercise 2: Chromatic Diminished Triad Inversions

This exercise will help build diminished triad recognition and performance through a strong rhythmic regimen. Practice the following exercise until it can be performed without hesitation.

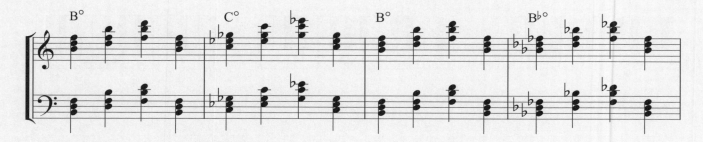

Diatonic Harmony

7

When each note of the major scale is harmonized in triads, a set of chords are created that represent *diatonic harmony*. This term refers to a group of chords that revolve around one key center or *tonic.* The chord that shares the same name as the major scale being harmonized is considered the tonic or *I* *("one")* chord.

C major (diatonic triads)

C	Dmi	Emi	F	G	Ami	B°	C
I	ii	iii	IV	V	vi	vii°	I
major	minor	minor	major	major	minor	diminished	major
tonic			subdominant	dominant			

As you can see from the above illustration, all the chord qualities we have studied so far (major, minor, and diminished) are used:

    3 major triads: *I, IV, V*

    3 minor triads: *ii, iii, vi*

    1 diminished triad: *vii°*

Note: *In this book, we will use upper case Roman numerals (I) to represent major, lower case (ii) to represent minor, and lower case followed by the diminished symbol (vii°) for diminished.*

Diatonic chord progressions are far and away the most commonly used device in popular music. Because of this, it is essential to understand the importance of the mood, movement, and relationship of these chords to their corresponding scale degrees.

The following progressions illustrate root position diatonic harmony for all major key centers. Play through each one, paying close attention to changing chord qualities and, of course, key signatures. Eventually, these progressions should be memorized.

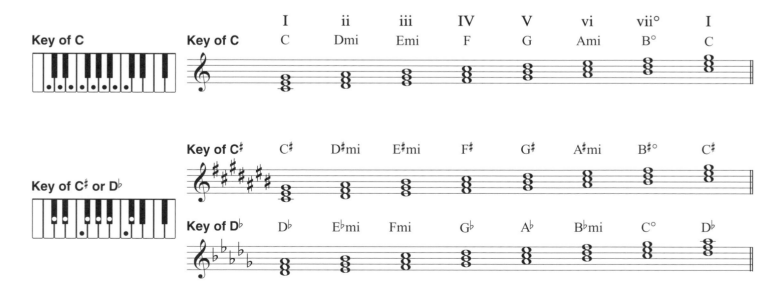

		I	ii	iii	IV	V	vi	vii°	I
Key of C	**Key of C**	C	Dmi	Emi	F	G	Ami	B°	C
Key of C♯ or D♭	**Key of C♯**	C♯	D♯mi	E♯mi	F♯	G♯	A♯mi	B♯°	C♯
	Key of D♭	D♭	E♭mi	Fmi	G♭	A♭	B♭mi	C°	D♭

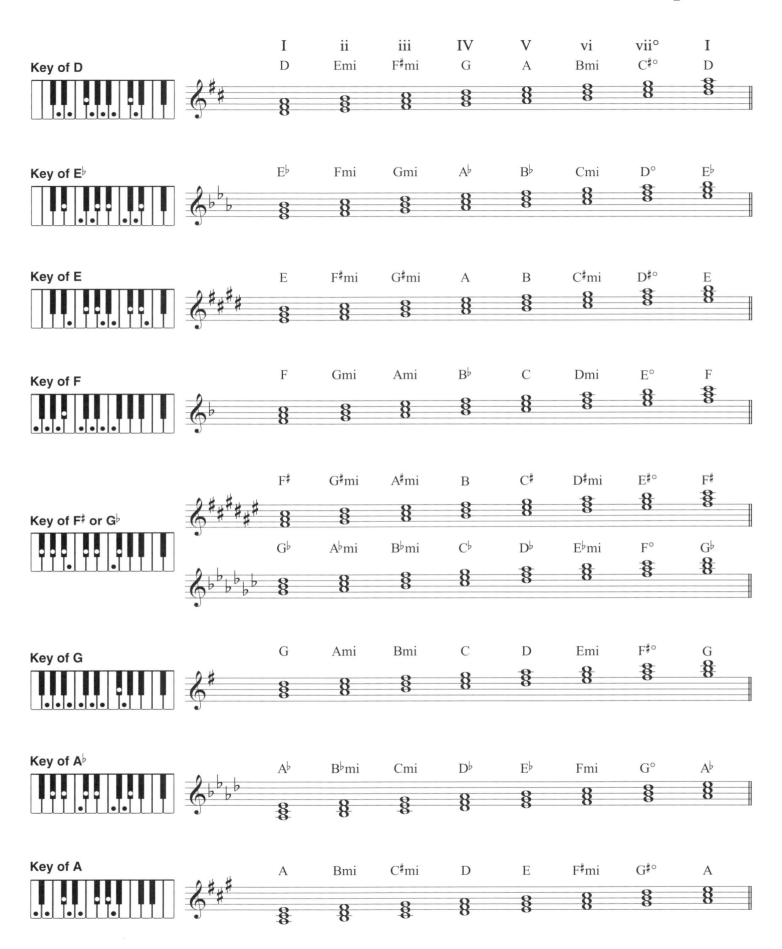

Chapter 7

Key of B♭

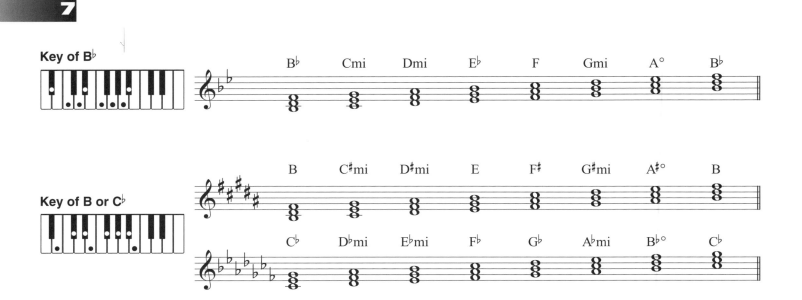

Key of B or C♭

Exercise: Popular Diatonic Chord Progressions

Locate and play the following progressions in the key of C. Then, try them in other keys, like G, F, and D major. Try to incorporate voice leading when possible. Also, attempt to verbalize the chord progression as you play it, saying both the letter name as well as the chord's quality.

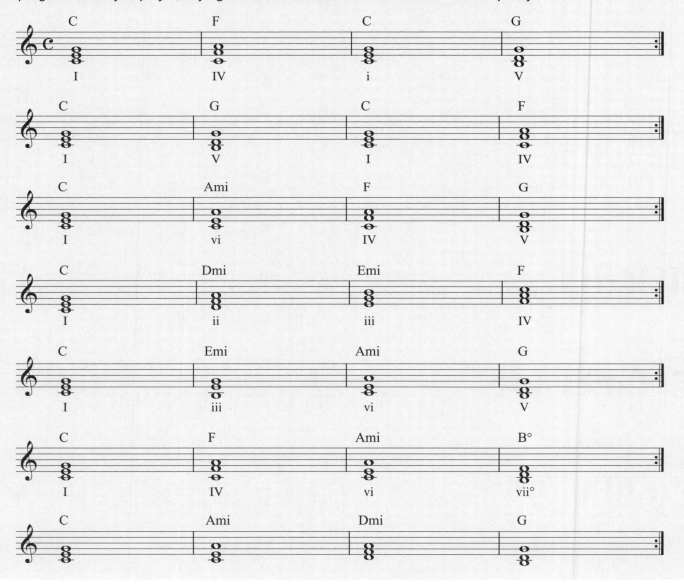

The Sus4 Chord

8

A suspended chord, or *sus* chord, is distinctly different from our previously learned triads in that it contains no 3rd. In essence, the term "sus," involves a particular pitch *replacing* the 3rd. The most common use of this device is when the *4th* scale degree is used instead of the 3rd. This is referred to as a *sus4* chord and causes the triad to sound less stable, or unresolved. Because it is the most commonly used suspension, many times only the "sus" suffix is used to imply a sus4. This unresolved quality can be relieved by the 4th *resolving* back to the 3rd, once again creating the triad. This "tension and release" effect is why the sus chord and the triad are used in succession to create harmonic movement on the same root.

Play the following progression to hear the "tension and release" effect of a suspended chord followed by the resolving triad:

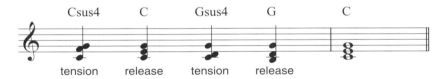

Here are all twelve sus4 chords and their inversions:

Csus4

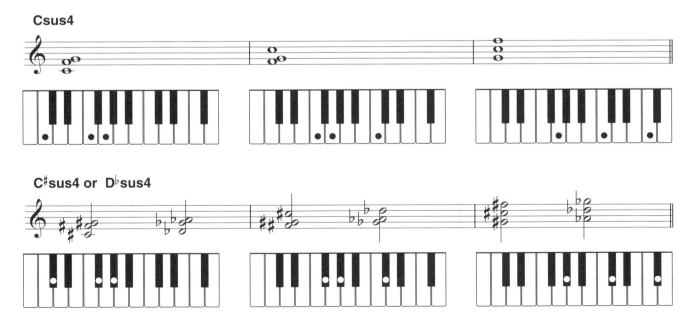

C♯sus4 or D♭sus4

Dsus4

D♯sus4 or E♭sus4

Esus4

Fsus4

F♯sus4 or G♭sus4

Gsus4

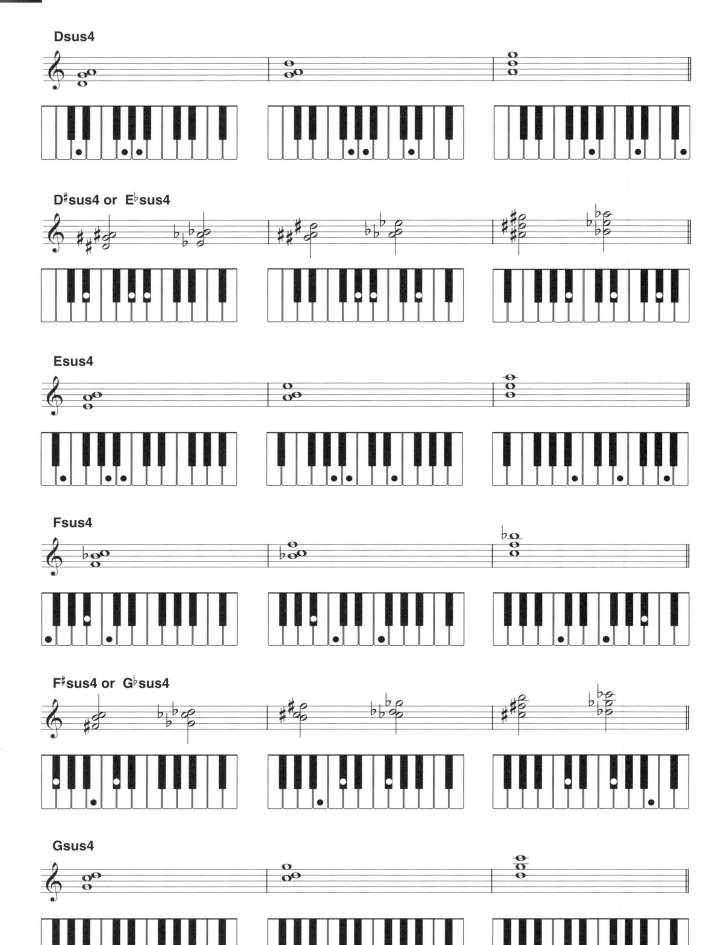

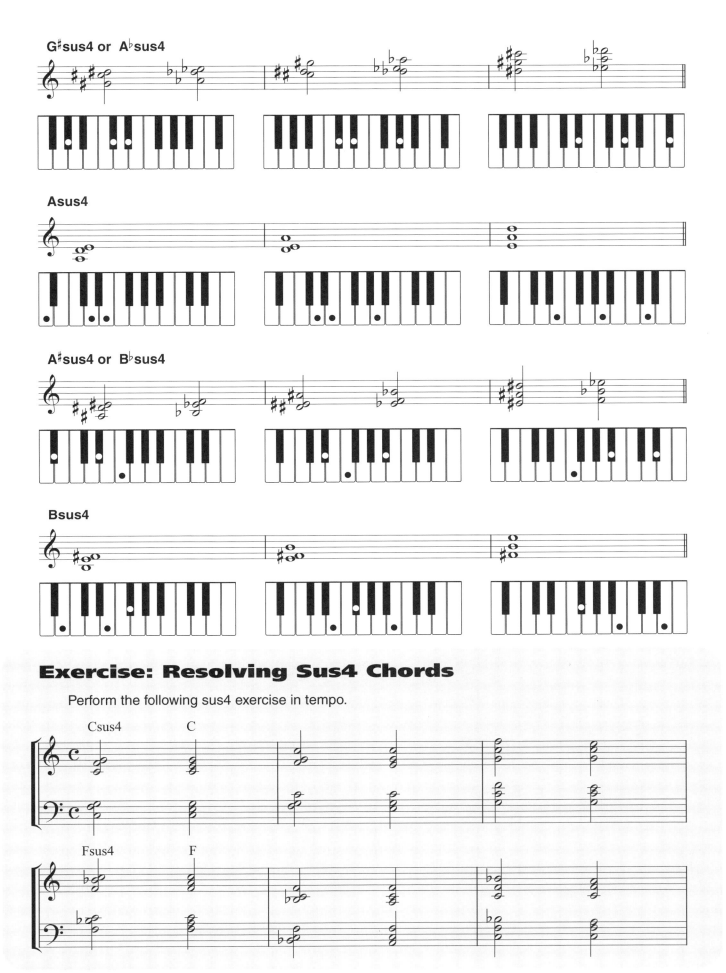

Exercise: Resolving Sus4 Chords

Perform the following sus4 exercise in tempo.

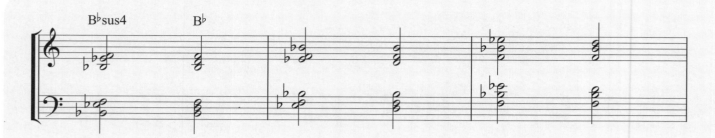

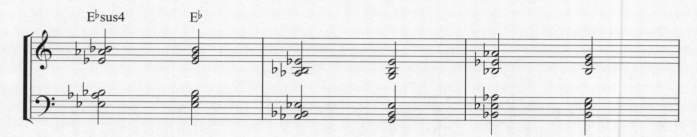

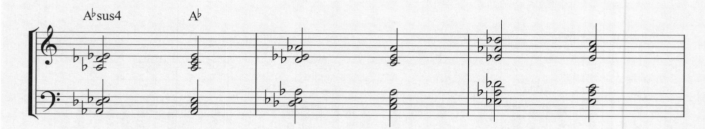

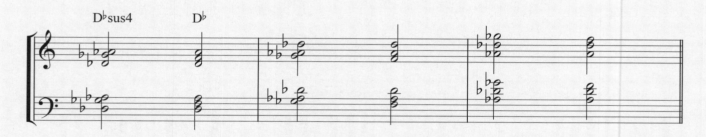

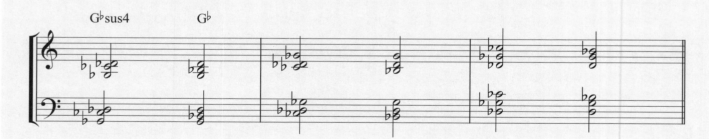

The Sus2 Chord

9

The *sus2* chord, like the sus4, contains no 3rd; the 3rd is now replaced by the 2nd, rather than the 4th. This chord is becoming more and more common in today's popular music. Because the 2nd is a whole step from the 3rd, its resolution to the triad is not as dramatic as the sus4's. Instead, the sus2 chord is used to "soften" the sound of the triad by making the quality unclear either momentarily or permanently. This chord, unlike the sus4, can produce a feeling of stability.

Perform the following examples to hear how sus chords can be used to vary a basic chord progression:

Chapter 9

Here are all twelve sus2 chords and their inversions:

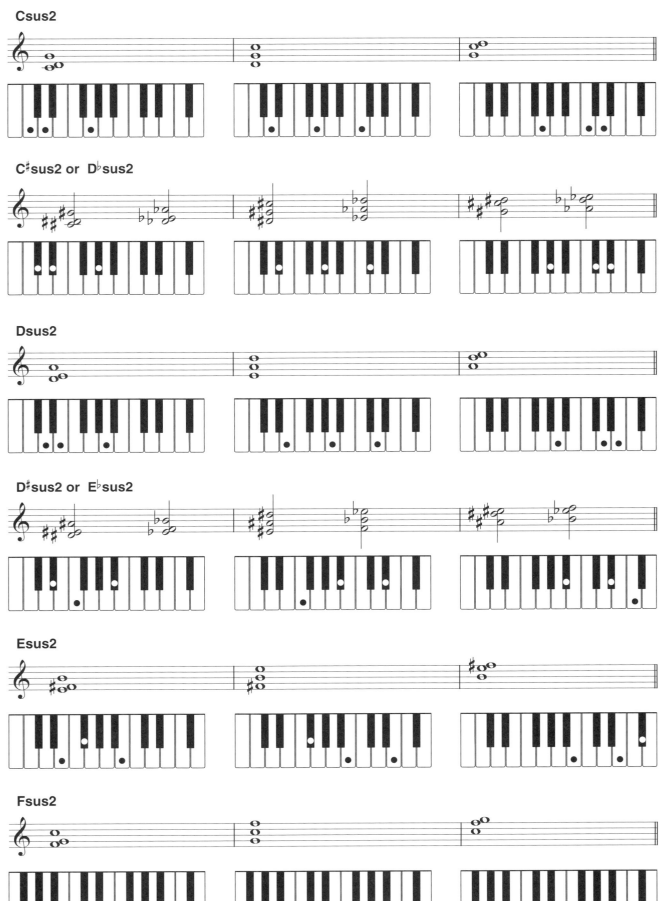

F#sus2 or G♭sus2

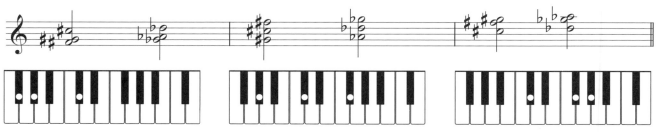

Gsus2

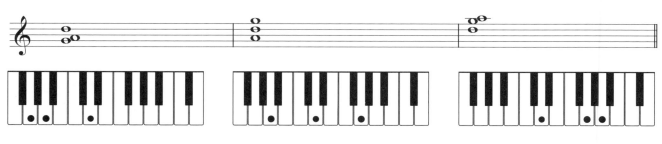

G#sus2 or A♭sus2

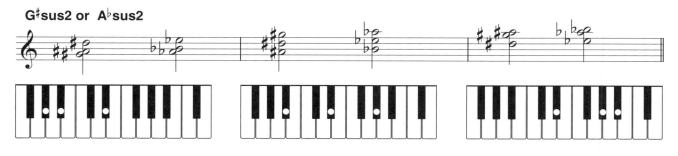

Asus2

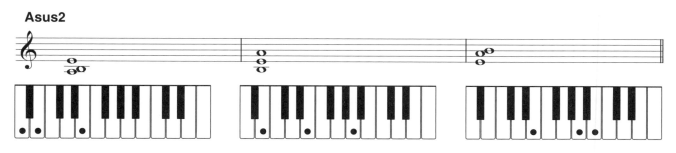

A#sus2 or B♭sus2

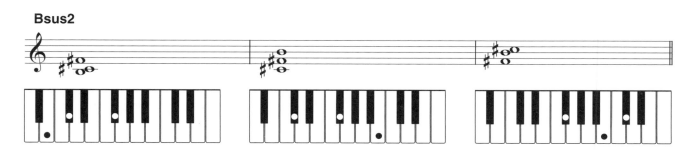

Bsus2

Exercise: Sus2 and Sus4 Chord Inversions

Perform the following sus2 exercise in tempo. Notice that the sus4 is also present in this progression.

The Augmented Triad

10

The last chord quality we must discuss before moving on to four-note chords is the *augmented* triad. Like the diminished triad, this chord's quality creates musical tension, or instability. In essence, this chord will always feel as if it needs to *resolve.* Also, the augmented triad does not use the same "shell." Because of this, it will have a slightly different shape and feel on the keyboard. The difference is that the 5th is *augmented* making it eight half steps above the root. To find the 5th of an augmented triad, count up eight half steps from the root, or simply raise the 5th of the major triad 1/2 step.

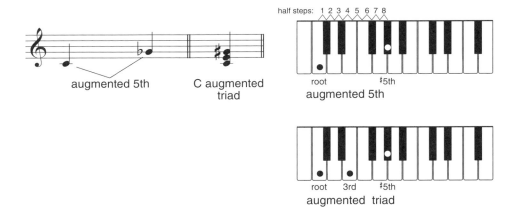

As you can see from the above illustration, the augmented triad uses the major 3rd and the augmented 5th intervals above the root. This triad is distinctive in that it is *symmetrical.* This is because the intervals between the root and the 3rd, and the 3rd and 5th are the same: a major 3rd (four half steps). Because of this, each inversion of the augmented triad will have the same construction:

The chord symbol for augmented is the letter name of the root followed by the symbol "+."

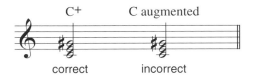

Here are all twelve augmented triads and their inversions:

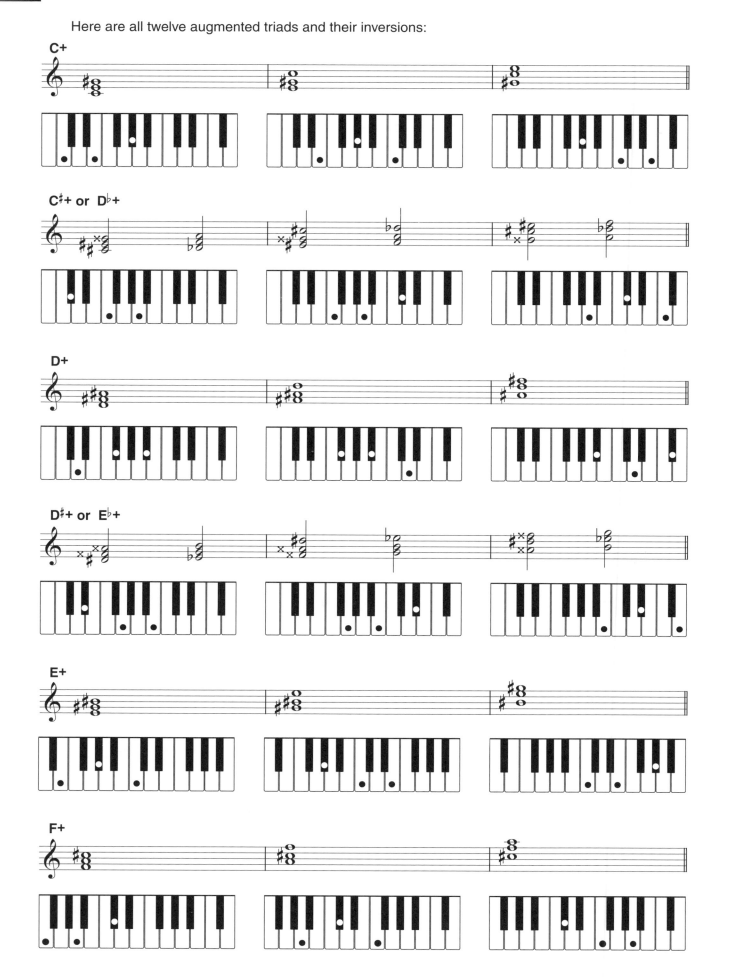

F#+ or G♭+

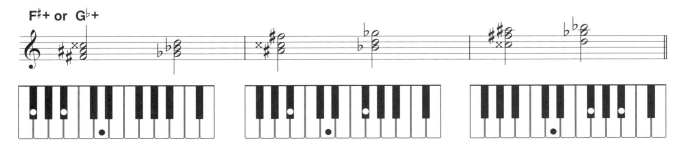

G+

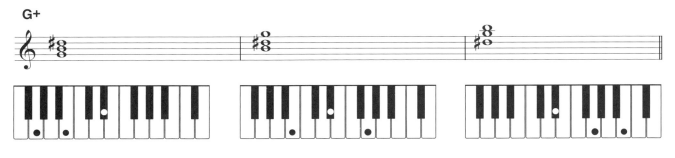

G#+ or A♭+

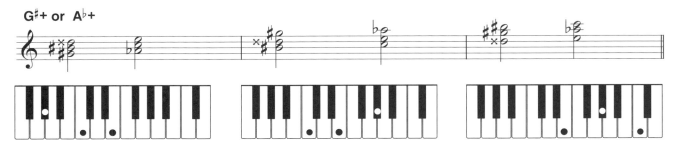

A+

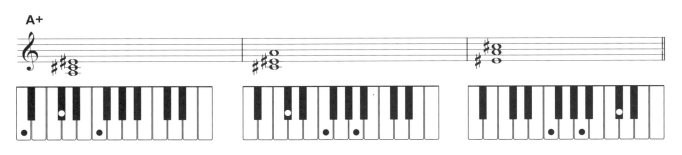

A#+ or B♭+

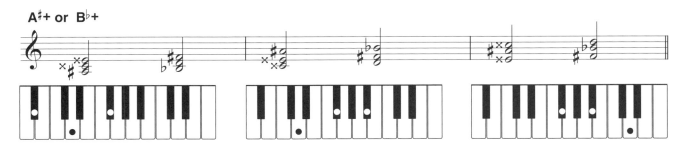

B+

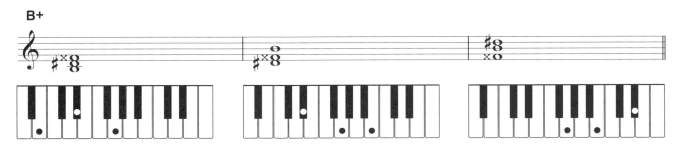

Exercise 1: Chromatic Augmented Triads

Locate and play all root position augmented triads by first arpeggiating the chord tones separately, immediately followed by the entire triad. Play the exercise with both hands, in tempo. Keep practicing this until it can be performed without hesitation.

Refer back to the illustrations on the previous page if necessary. As you practice this exercise, begin to internalize the sound of the augmented "quality." Again, attempt to get a feel for this shape as well as a mental picture of the note groupings.

Exercise 2: Augmented Voice Leading

Perform the following augmented triad voice-leading exercise.

Congratulations! You have just completed an exhaustive study of all three-note chord qualities and their inversions. If you have completed all drills in these first ten chapters, you are ready to proceed to larger and more complex chords. It is important to understand that all upcoming information is based on your complete understanding of the previous chapters. Therefore, do not hesitate to continue using these drills in your daily practice regimen.

By now you should have begun to internalize these chords visually, sonically, and physically. If this has occurred, adding additional chord tones to these pre-existing shapes will help build your chord vocabulary quickly and efficiently.

The Major Seventh Chord

11

The *major seventh* chord consists of a major triad with the addition of the note a major 7th above the tonic. The addition of this *leading tone* immediately adds more complexity and color to the simplicity of the major triad. If you are not already familiar with this chord's sonic character, you might classify its sonority as "jazzy." As we begin to insert these new chord qualities into various musical style, you will soon recognize that the major seventh quality is found in many types of genres other than jazz, and can be used as an alternative to the simplicity of the major triad.

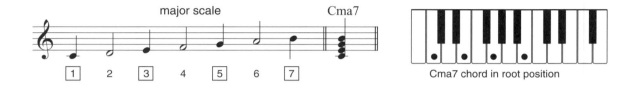

Cma7 chord in root position

There are a variety of chord symbols used to notate the major seventh. The one used above (ma7) is probably the most widely used and considered to be the clearest notation of this quality. Here are a few other types you might see:

Like all the chord symbols discussed earlier, the suffix which describes the quality must be preceded by the letter name of the chord's root. Because of the popular usage of slash chord notation, we must also be able to recognize the major seventh when it is notated this way:

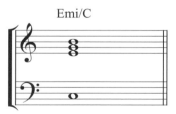

Although this is not the recommended notation, this is an accurate description of this chord's construction. The understanding that the 3rd, 5th, and 7th of this chord (E, G, and B) construct a separate minor triad, above the bass, could prove to be a valuable tool.

Here are all the major seventh chords in root position:

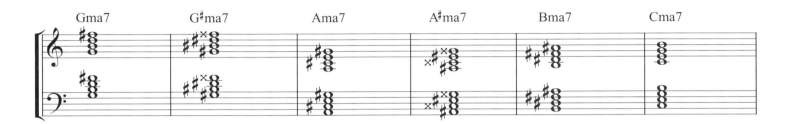

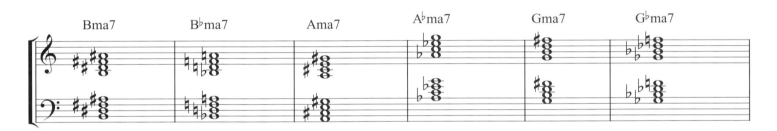

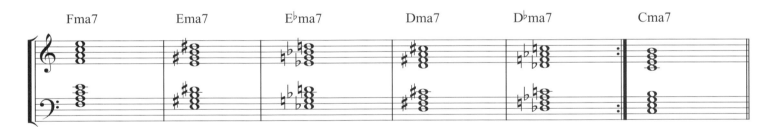

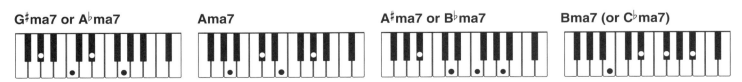

Cma7

C♯ma7 or D♭ma7

Dma7

D♯ma7 or E♭ma7

Ema7

Fma7

F♯ma7 or G♭ma7

Gma7

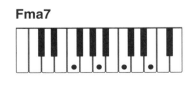

G♯ma7 or A♭ma7

Ama7

A♯ma7 or B♭ma7

Bma7 (or C♭ma7)

Inversions

Now that we are constructing four-note chords, there is an additional inversion needed. This inversion, known as *third* inversion, is when the *7th* is found in the bottom of the chord.

single-hand voicing or "closed":

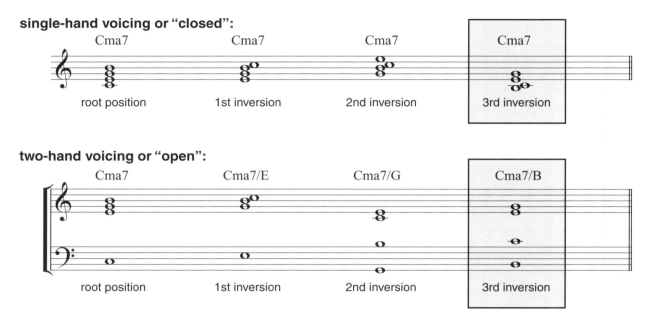

two-hand voicing or "open":

As with our triad study, it is essential that you become equally familiar with all of these inversions. In achieving this skill, the player will be able to easily incorporate voice leading into performance.

Throughout this book, we will concentrate on the "rootless" voicing. This will prepare the student to omit tones that are nonessential to a chord's quality of color. As chord construction becomes more complex, some chord tones should be omitted to retain clarity. The "rootless" voicing is the playing of all essential chord tones in a single hand, while omitting the root. In the following exercises, the left hand will take on the role of bass player, playing only the root of the chord. The right hand will play the remaining three chord tones. For example:

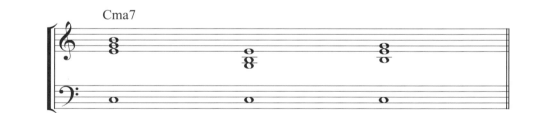

Exercise 1

Perform the following major seventh drill in tempo. Notice how voice leading is used to create smooth transitions.

Exercise 2

Perform the following exercise in tempo. Notice the "rootless" voicing in the left hand, with a simple melody in the right.

The Minor Seventh Chord

The *minor seventh* chord consists of a minor triad plus the note a minor 7th above the tonic. The addition of this "subtonic" immediately adds more color and density to the simplicity of the minor triad. This chord quality may be the most commonly used chord sound in all of contemporary music, and can serve as an alternative to the simplicity of the minor triad.

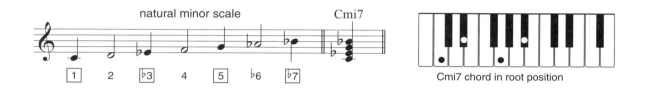

Cmi7 chord in root position

There are a variety of chord symbols used to notate the minor seventh. The one above (mi7) is probably the most widely used and is considered to be the clearest notation of this quality. Here are a few other types you might see:

Like all the chord symbols discussed earlier, the suffix which describes the quality must be preceded by the letter name of the chord's root. Because of the popular usage of slash chord notation, we must also be able to recognize the minor seventh when it is notated this way:

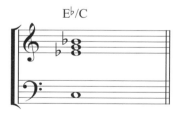

Although this is not the recommended notation, this is an accurate description of this chord's construction. The understanding that the 3rd, 5th, and 7th of this chord (E♭, G, and B♭) construct a separate major triad, above the bass, could prove to be a valuable tool.

Here are all the minor seventh chords in root position:

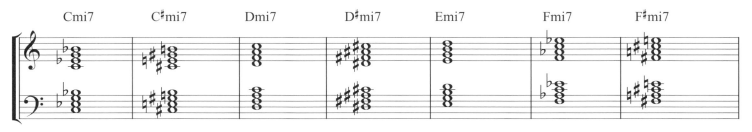

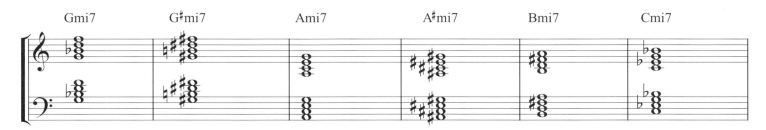

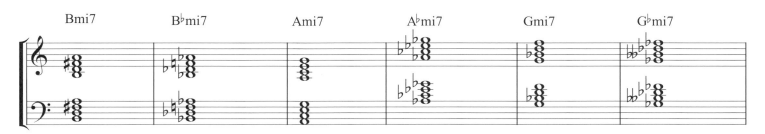

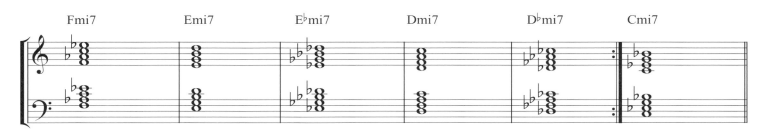

Cmi7

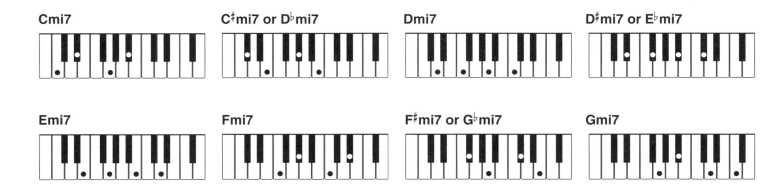

C#mi7 or D♭mi7

Dmi7

D#mi7 or E♭mi7

Emi7

Fmi7

F#mi7 or G♭mi7

Gmi7

G#mi7 or A♭mi7

Ami7

A#mi7 or B♭mi7

Bmi7 or C♭mi7

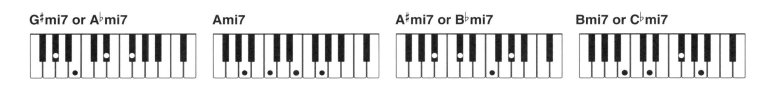

Inversions

single-hand voicing or "closed":

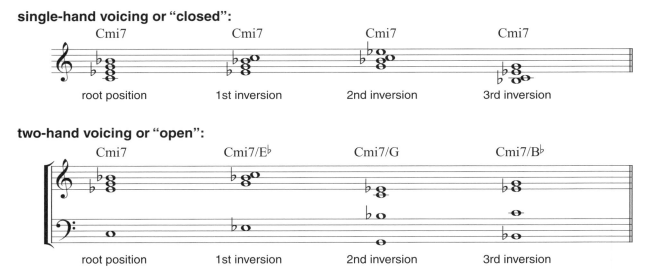

root position   1st inversion   2nd inversion   3rd inversion

two-hand voicing or "open":

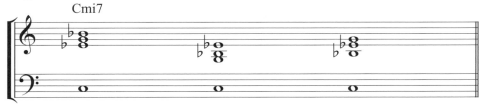

root position   1st inversion   2nd inversion   3rd inversion

"rootless" voicings:

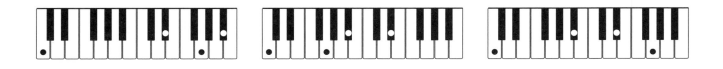

Exercise 1

Perform the following minor seventh drill in tempo. Notice how voice leading is used to create smooth transitions.

Exercise 2

Perform the following exercise in tempo. Notice the "rootless" voicing in the left hand, with a simple melody in the right. Practice hands separately at first, if necessary.

The Dominant
13 Seventh Chord

The *dominant seventh* chord consists of a major triad with the addition of the note a minor 7th above the tonic. Within this shape is the diminished 5th interval, or tritone, which creates a feeling of instability. This chord is used primarily to enhance the arrival of a stable, resolved chord. As the name suggests, the dominant seventh usually functions as a V7 chord. One musical situation that completely contradicts this stereotype is blues harmony, where the dominant seventh functions as a I chord, feeling stable and complete.

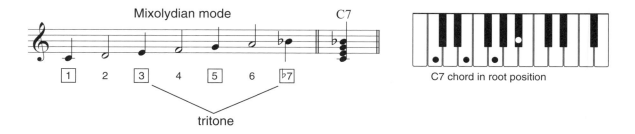

C7 chord in root position

It is essential to be aware of the importance of this tritone shape, as it defines the character of the dominant seventh. In general, the importance of 3rd and 7th understanding in any chord cannot be overstated, and becomes vital in further study of chord voicing.

Note: *This is the only seventh chord quality that uses the number (C7) directly after the letter name of the root. No prefix is needed as in the ma7 and mi7.*

Because of the popular usage of slash chord notation, we must also be able to recognize the dominant seventh when it is noted this way:

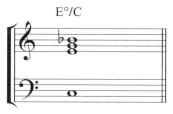

Although this is not the recommended notation, this is an accurate description of this chord's construction. The understanding that the 3rd, 5th, and 7th of this chord (E, G, and B♭) construct a separate diminished triad, above the bass, could prove to be a valuable tool.

Here are all the dominant seventh chords in root position:

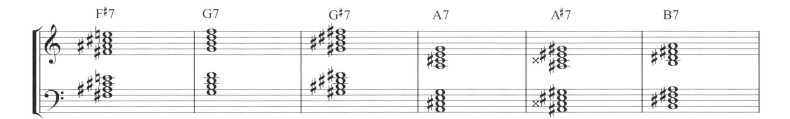

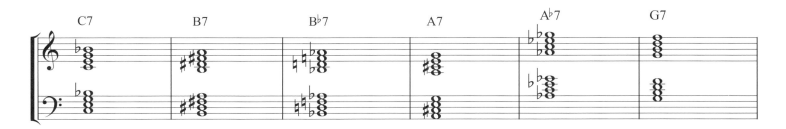

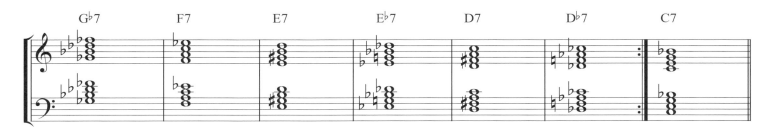

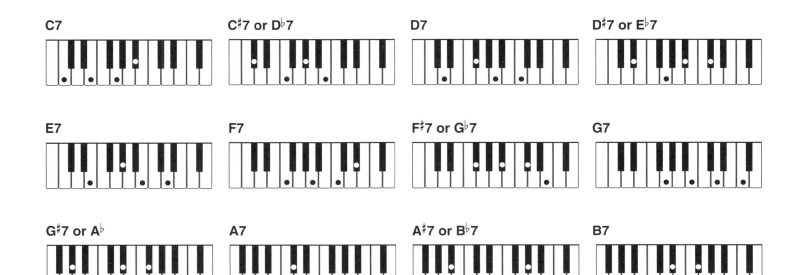

Inversions

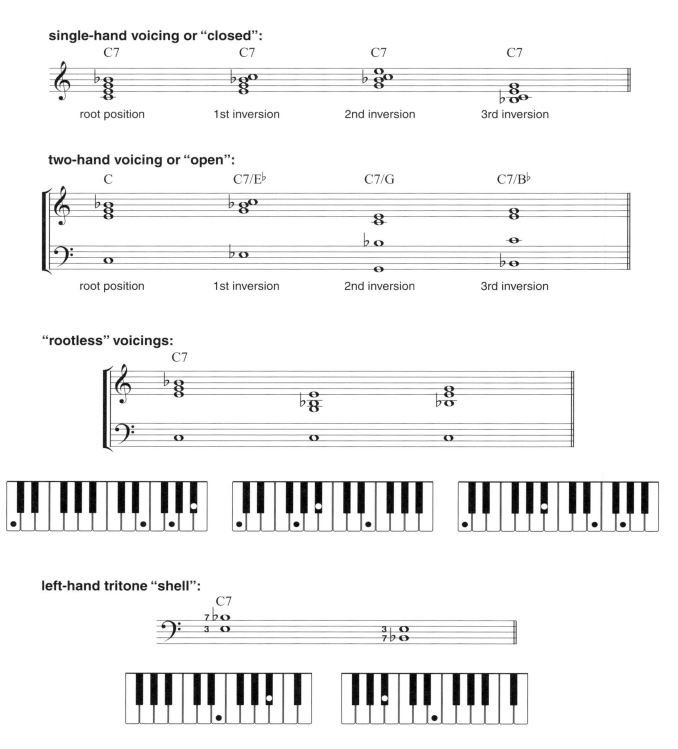

single-hand voicing or "closed":

root position 1st inversion 2nd inversion 3rd inversion

two-hand voicing or "open":

root position 1st inversion 2nd inversion 3rd inversion

"rootless" voicings:

left-hand tritone "shell":

As you can see, the tritone shell omits the use of the 5th, leaving room for later extension or alteration. This will become common practice with all chords once they are extended past the 7th. To explore this further, try performing Exercise 2 from Chapters 11 and 12 with simple shells (3rd and 7th only). This can be done by simply omitting the 5th from the left hand voicing. You will hear that there is very little difference in character (which is why the 5th is not missed when deleted).

Exercise 1

Perform the following dominant seventh drill in tempo. Notice how voice leading is used to create smooth transitions.

Exercise 2

Perform the following exercise in tempo. Notice the "tritone-shell" voicings in the left hand, with a simple melody in the right. Practice hands separately at first if necessary.

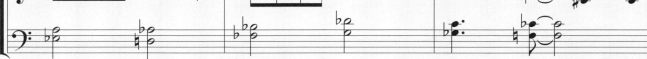

The Minor Seven
14 Flat-Five Chord

The *minor seven flat-five* or *half diminished* chord, consists of a diminished triad with the addition of the note a minor 7th above the tonic. Because of its diminished quality, it produces an unstable effect which needs to resolve. This chord quality most commonly functions as a ii chord in a minor key, but can also substitute for IV or VI in minor, or for V7 in major.

There are a variety of chord symbols used to notate the minor seven flat-five. The one used above (mi7♭5), is probably the most widely used and considered to be the clearest notation of this quality. Here are a few other types you might see:

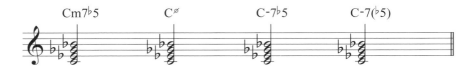

Because of the popular usage of "slash chord" notation, we must also be able to recognize the minor seven flat-five when it is notated this way:

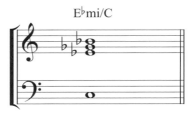

Although this is not the recommended notation, this is an accurate description of this chord's construction. The understanding that the 3rd, 5th, and 7th of this chord (E♭, G♭, and B♭) construct a separate minor triad, above the bass, could prove to be a valuable tool.

Here are all the minor seven flat-five chords in root position:

Inversions

single-hand voicing or "closed":

root position   1st inversion   2nd inversion   3rd inversion

two-hand voicing or "open":

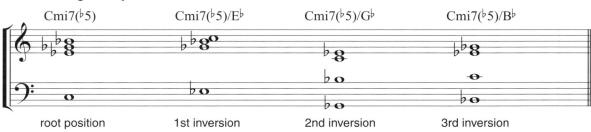

root position   1st inversion   2nd inversion   3rd inversion

"rootless" voicings:

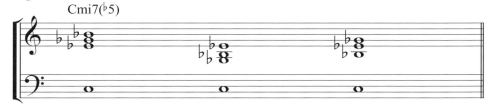

Exercise 1

Perform the following minor seven flat-five drill in tempo. Notice how voice leading is used to create smooth transitions.

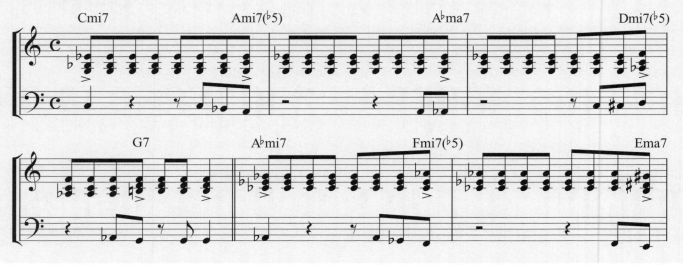

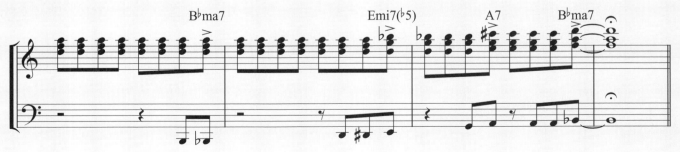

The Dominant Seven
15 Sharp-Five Chord

The *dominant seven sharp-five,* or *augmented seventh* chord, consists of an augmented triad with the addition of the note a minor 7th above the tonic. This chord usually functions as a V7 chord. It can be used to create even a stronger pull toward the tonic than the previously learned dominant seventh because of the urgency of the augmented 5th to resolve.

There are a variety of chord symbols used to notate the dominant seven sharp-five. The one used above (7♯5) is probably the most widely used and considered to be the clearest notation of this quality. Here are a few other types you might see:

Because of the popular usage of slash chord notation, we must also be able to recognize the dominant seven sharp-five when it is notated this way:

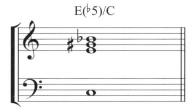

Although this is not the recommended notation, this is an accurate description of this chord's construction. The understanding that the 3rd, 5th, and 7th of this chord (E, G♯, and B♭) construct a separate altered major triad, above the bass, could prove to be a valuable tool.

Here are all the dominant seven sharp-five chords in root position:

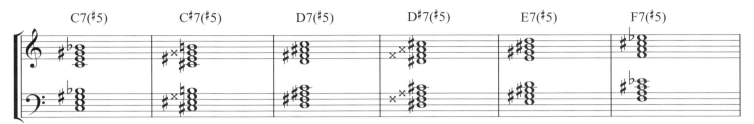

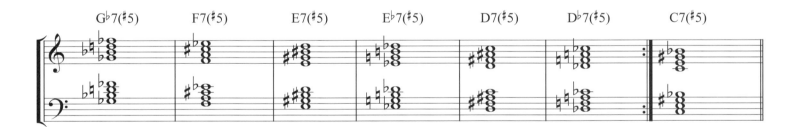

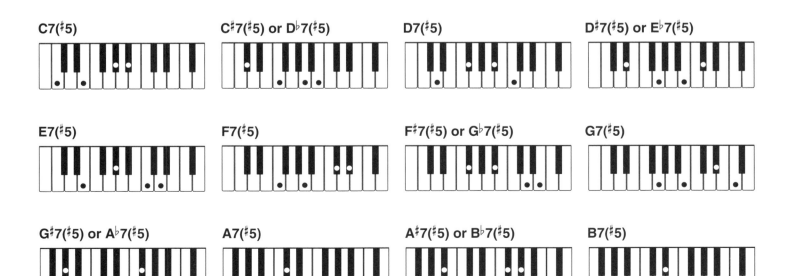

Inversions

single-hand voicing or "closed":

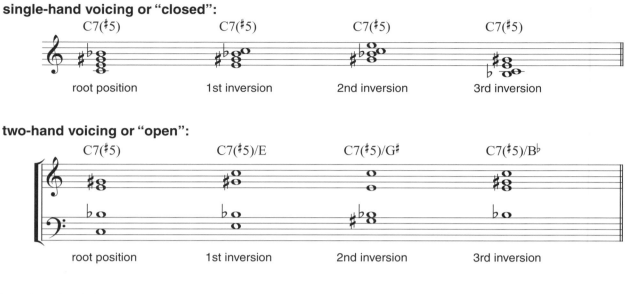

two-hand voicing or "open":

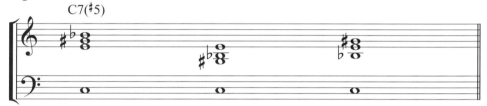

"rootless" voicings:

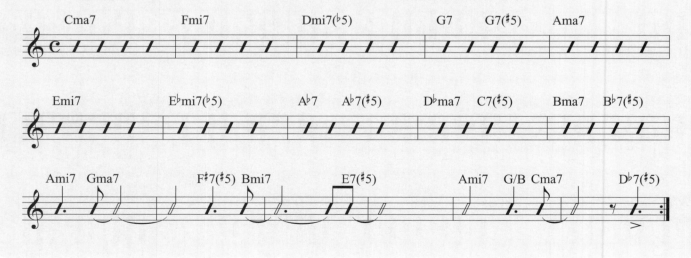

Exercise 1

Perform the following chord progression in tempo. Incorporate "rootless" voicings, voice leading, and the style of your choice. Be able to play this exercise with either hand separately.

Exercise 2

While playing rootless voicings in the left hand, add this melody in the right.

The Diminished
16 Seventh Chord

The *diminished seventh,* or *fully diminished,* chord consists of a diminished triad with the addition of the diminished 7th note (major 6th) above the tonic. Because of its diminished quality, this chord produces an unstable effect which needs to resolve. This chord quality most commonly functions as the vii°7 of the chord that follows it, in essence functioning like a dominant chord. Otherwise, the diminished seventh chord is used as a passing chord in chromatic harmony.

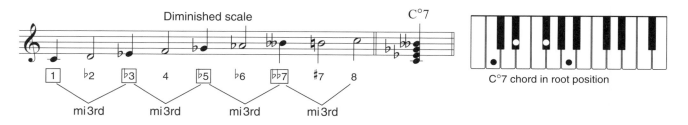

C°7 chord in root position

As you can see from the above illustration, the diminished seventh chord is constructed of successive minor 3rd intervals, thus dividing the octave into four equal parts. This symmetrical shape is important to recognize because each fully diminished chord must fall into one of only three possible constructions:

Group 1: C°, D#° or E♭°, F#° or G♭°, and A°

Group 2: C#° or D♭°, E°, G°, and A#° or B♭°

Group 3: D°, F°, G#° or A♭°, and B°

Every diminished seventh chord within the same group shares the *exact same chord tones!*

Here are the two chord symbols you will see to notate this chord:

Here are all the diminished seventh chords in root position:

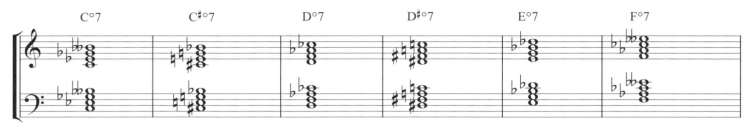

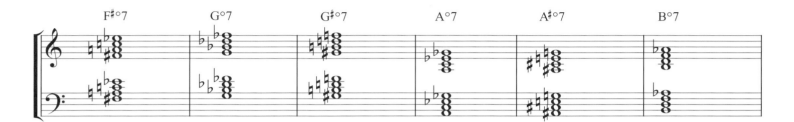

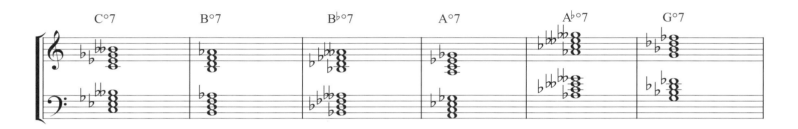

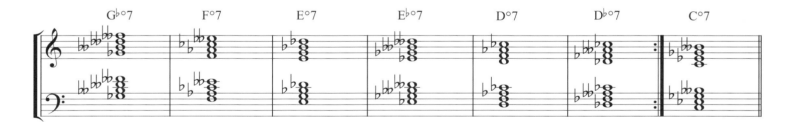

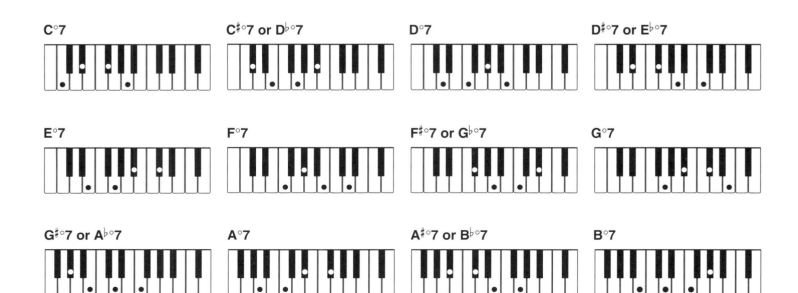

Inversions

Here are the three groups discussed in the beginning of this chapter:

Technically, there are no inversions of diminished seventh chords. Whatever note appears in the bass will be considered the chord's letter name.

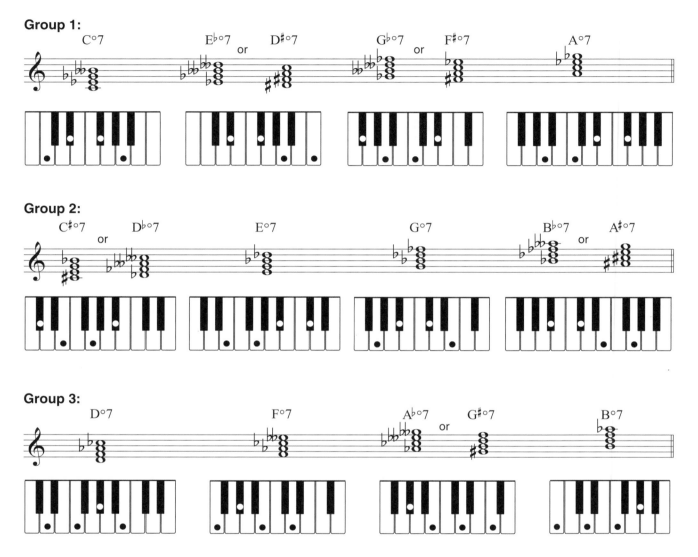

Group 1:

Group 2:

Group 3:

As you can see from the illustration above, it would be redundant to label a chord C°7/E♭ because C°7 and E♭°7 contain the same chord tones. Because of this, all diminished seventh chords will be interpreted in root position.

Chapter 16

Exercise 1

Perform the following chord progression in tempo. Incorporate "rootless" voicings and voice leading. Be able to play this exercise with either hand separately.

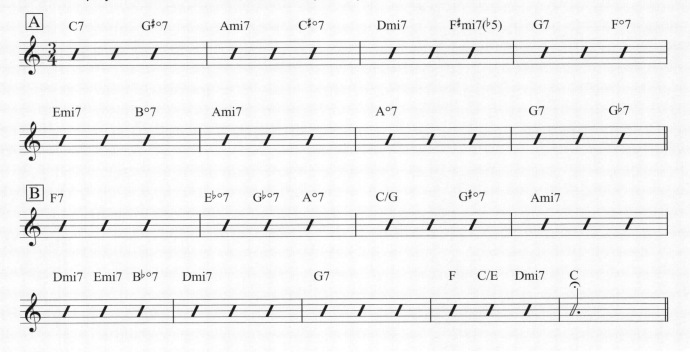

Use this voicing example to prepare yourself for performance of the next exercise.

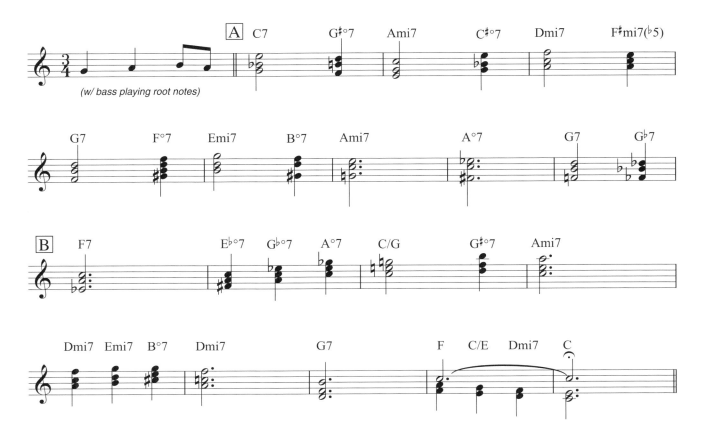

Exercise 2

Perform the following song with bass note in the left hand and the melody in the top of the "rootless" voicing. Be sure not to double the root when playing this exercise unless it appears in the melody.

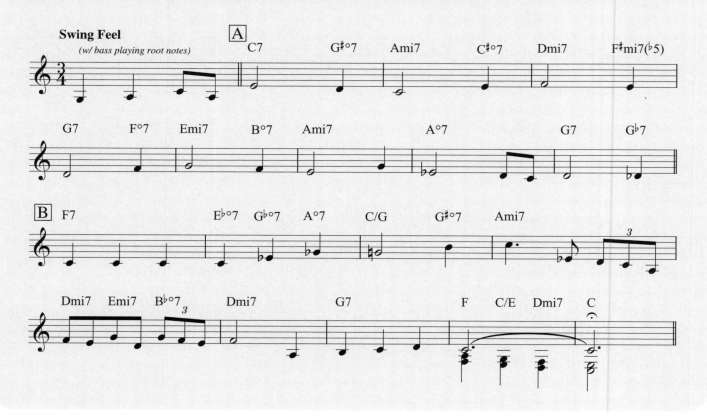

The Dominant Seven Flat-Five Chord

17

The dominant seven flat-five chord is constructed much like the dominant seventh except that, as the name implies, the 5th of the chord is lowered 1/2 step. This chord usually functions as a ♭II7 chord or tritone substitution. In other words, it is commonly substituted for the dominant seventh chord a tritone (augmented 4th or diminished 5th) away, which is usually functioning as a V7 chord. This ♭II7 substitution can be used to create stronger pull toward the tonic, caused by the chromatic bass line.

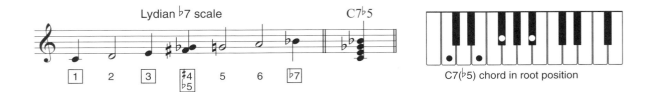

Here are the two chord symbols you will see to notate this chord:

Because of the popular usage of slash chord notation, we must also be able to recognize the dominant seven flat-five when it is notated this way:

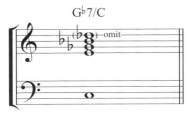

Although this is not the recommended notation, this is an accurate description of this chord's construction. The understanding that the dominant seventh chord built a tritone above or below the root will effectively construct the 7♭5 could prove to be a valuable tool.

Here are all the dominant seven flat-five chords in root position:

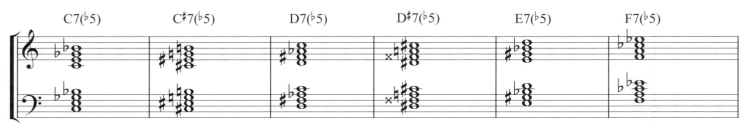

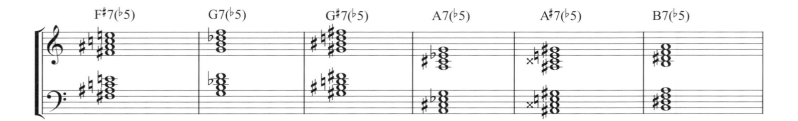

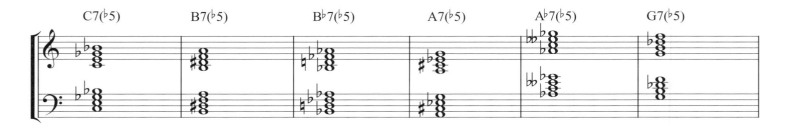

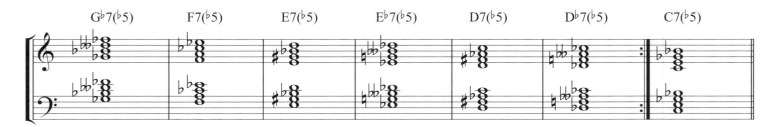

C7(♭5)

C♯7(♭5) or D♭7(♭5)

D7(♭5)

D♯7(♭5) or E♭7(♭5)

E7(♭5)

F7(♭5)

F♯7♭5 or G♭7(♭5)

G7(♭5)

G♯7(♭5) or A♭7(♭5)

A7(♭5)

A♯7(♭5) or B♭7(♭5)

B7(♭5)

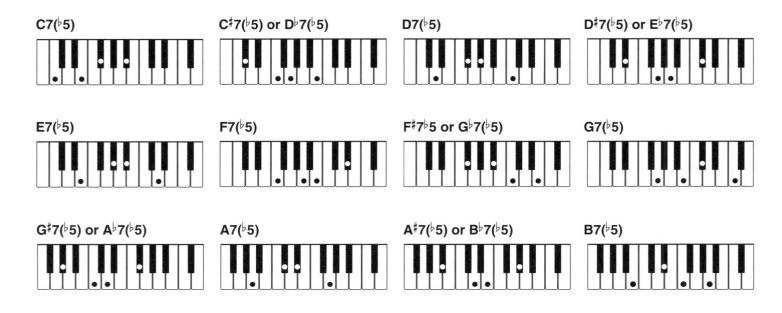

Chapter 17

Inversions

single-hand voicing or "closed":

two-hand voicing or "open":

"rootless" voicings:

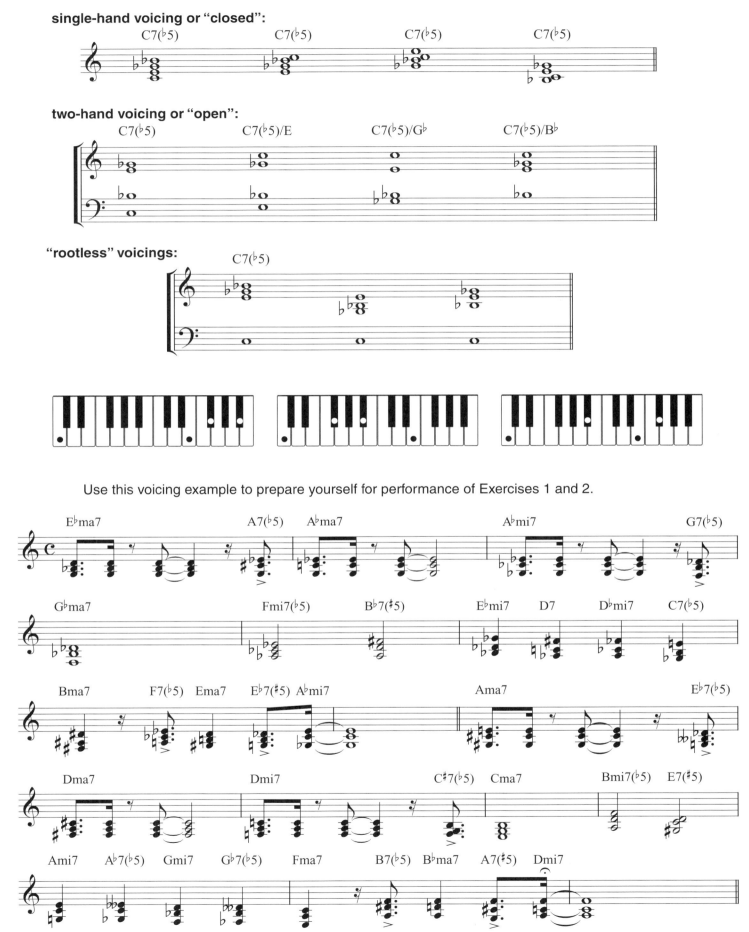

Use this voicing example to prepare yourself for performance of Exercises 1 and 2.

Exercise 1

Perform the following chord progression in tempo. Incorporate "rootless" voicings and voice leading. Be able to play this exercise with either hand separately.

Exercise 2

While playing rootless voicings in the left hand, add this melody in the right.

The Dominant 7sus4 Chord

18

The *dominant 7sus4 chord* consists of a sus4 triad with the addition of the note a minor 7th above the tonic. As you know from previous studies, the suspended 4th or "sus4" replaces the third of the triad thus creating an unresolved sound. The 7sus4 is commonly followed by the dominant seventh of the same name, which resolves the 4 to the 3. Because the dominant seventh itself is somewhat unstable, the use of the suspension (4 to 3) merely extends the anticipation created by the dominant quality. It is also very common for the 7sus4 to remain unresolved, never using the 3rd at all.

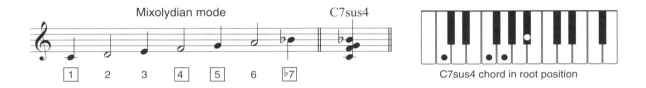

Here are the chord symbols you will see to notate this chord:

Because of the popular usage of slash chord notation, we must also be able to recognize the dominant 7sus4 chord when it is notated this way:

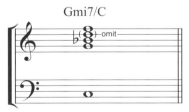

Although this is not the recommended notation, this is an accurate description of this chord's construction. The understanding that the minor seventh chord built a perfect 5th above the root will effectively construct the 7sus4 could prove to be a valuable tool. (The 5th of the minor seventh chord could be retained if the 9sus4 is desired.)

Here are all the dominant 7sus4 chords in root position:

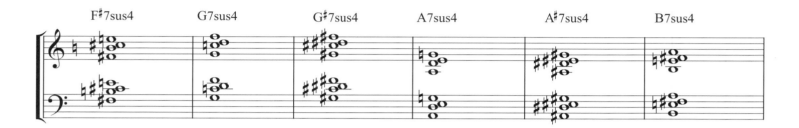

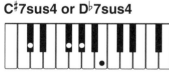

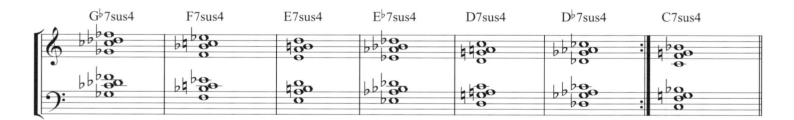

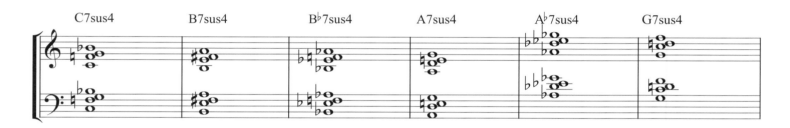

C7sus4

C#7sus4 or D♭7sus4

D7sus4

D#7sus4 or E♭7sus4

E7sus4

F7sus4

F#7sus4 or G♭7sus4

G7sus4

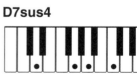

G#7sus4 or A♭7sus4

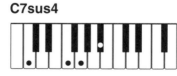

A7sus4

A#7sus4 or B♭7sus4

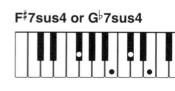

B7sus4

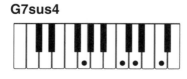

Chapter 18

Inversions

single-hand voicing or "closed":

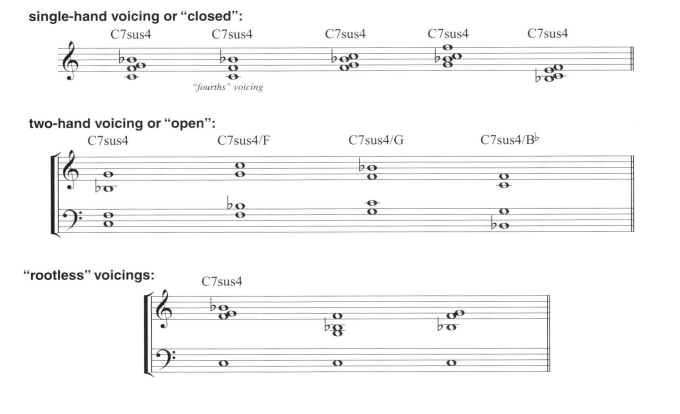

"fourths" voicing

two-hand voicing or "open":

"rootless" voicings:

Use this voicing example to prepare yourself for performance of Exercises 1 and 2.

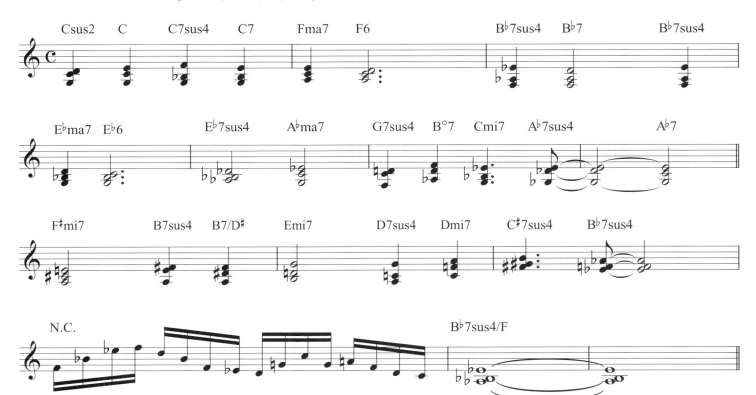

Exercise 1

Perform the following chord progression in tempo. Incorporate "rootless" voicings and voice leading. Be able to play this exercise with either hand separately.

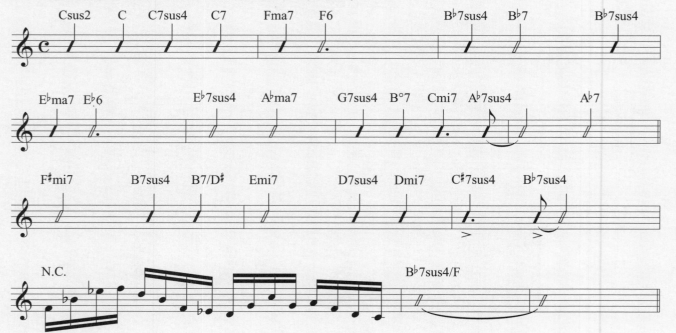

Exercise 2

While playing rootless voicings in the left hand, add this melody in the right hand.

The Minor-Major Seventh Chord

19

The *minor-major seventh* chord consists of a minor triad with the addition of the note a major 7th above the tonic. The addition of this "leading tone" above the minor triad causes a distinct dissonance that is commonly used for effect at the end of a song. This chord is also commonly used to create movement between the root of the minor chord and its major 6th, thus creating a descending chromatic bass line. The tune "This Masquerade," made famous by guitarist George Benson, uses this device.

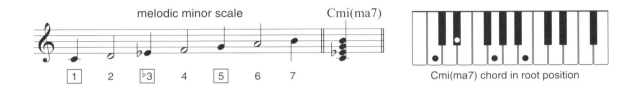

Cmi(ma7) chord in root position

There are a variety of chord symbols used to notate the minor-major seventh chord. Here are a few other types you might see:

Because of the popular usage of slash chord notation, we must also be able to recognize the minor-major seventh chord when it is notated this way:

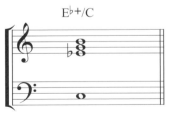

Although this is not the recommended notation, this is an accurate description of this chord's construction. The understanding that the 3rd, 5th, and 7th of this chord (E♭, G, and B) construct a separate augmented triad, above the bass, could prove to be a valuable tool.

Here are all the minor-major seventh chords in root position:

Inversions

single-hand voicing or "closed":

two-hand voicing or "open":

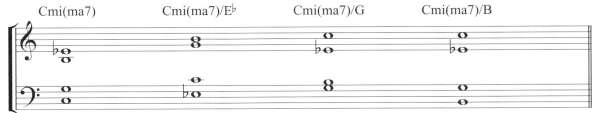

"rootless" voicings:

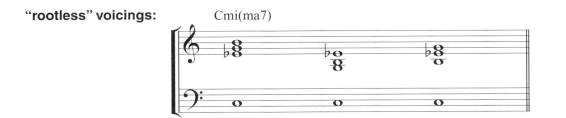

Use this voicing example to prepare yourself for performance of Exercises 1 and 2.

Exercise 1

Perform the following chord progression in tempo. Incorporate "rootless" voicings and voice leading. Be able to play this exercise with either hand separately.

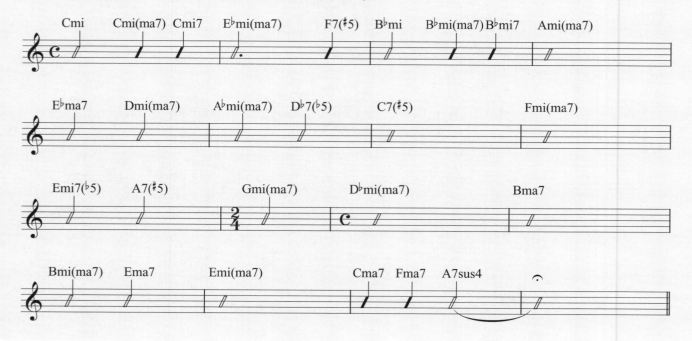

Exercise 2

While playing rootless voicings in the left hand, add this melody in the right.

The Major Seven
20 Flat-Five Chord

The *major seven flat-five* chord is constructed by simply lowering the 5th of a major seventh chord by a half step. The tritone that is created between the root and the diminished 5th gives this chord a distinct sound that is commonly used as a IV chord in a major key and a VI chord in minor. However, unlike the diminished and half-diminished chord qualities, which also contain the tritone above the root, this chord remains relatively bright because of the major 3rd and 7th.

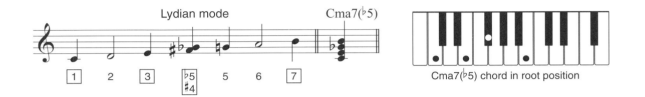

Here are the two chord symbols you will see to notate this chord:

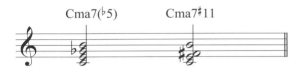

Because of the popular usage of slash chord notation, we must also be able to recognize the major seven flat-five chord when it is notated this way:

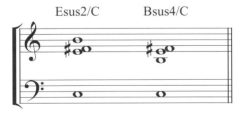

Although this is not the recommended notation, this is an accurate description of this chord's construction. The understanding that the 3rd, 5th, and 7th of this chord (E, G♭, and B) construct a separate suspended triad, above the bass, could prove to be a valuable tool.

Here are all the major seven flat-five chords in root position:

Inversions

single-hand voicing or "closed":

two-hand voicing or "open":

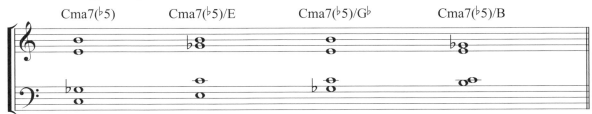

"rootless" voicings:

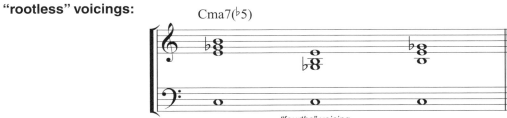

"fourths" voicing

Use this voicing example to prepare yourself for performance of Exercises 1 and 2.

Exercise 1

Perform the following chord progression in tempo. Incorporate "rootless" voicings and voice leading. Be able to play this exercise with either hand separately.

Exercise 2

While playing rootless voicings in the left hand, add this melody in the right.

MUSICIANS INSTITUTE

Press

Musicians Institute Press

is the official series of Southern California's renowned music school, Musicians Institute. **MI** instructors, some of the finest musicians in the world, share their vast knowledge and experience with you – no matter what your current level. For guitar, bass, drums, vocals, and keyboards, **MI Press** offers the finest music curriculum for higher learning through a variety of series:

ESSENTIAL CONCEPTS
Designed from MI core curriculum programs.

MASTER CLASS
Designed from MI elective courses.

PRIVATE LESSONS
Tackle a variety of topics "one-on-one" with MI faculty instructors.

FOR MORE INFORMATION, SEE YOUR LOCAL MUSIC DEALER,
OR WRITE TO:

HAL•LEONARD®
CORPORATION

7777 W. BLUEMOUND RD. P.O. BOX 13819 MILWAUKEE, WI 53213

Prices, contents, and availability subject to change without notice. Some products may not be available outside of the U.S.A.

GUITAR

Advanced Scale Concepts & Licks for Guitar
by Jean Marc Belkadi
Private Lessons
00695298 Book/CD Pack $12.95

Basic Blues Guitar
by Steve Trovato
Private Lessons
00695180 Book/CD Pack $12.95

Creative Chord Shapes
by Jamie Findlay
Private Lessons
00695172 Book/CD Pack $7.95

Diminished Scale for Guitar
by Jean Marc Belkadi
Private Lessons
00695227 Book/CD Pack $9.95

Guitar Basics
by Bruce Buckingham
Private Lessons
00695134 Book/CD Pack $14.95

Guitar Hanon
by Peter Deneff
Private Lessons
00695321 . . . . $9.95

Guitar Soloing
by Dan Gilbert & Beth Marlis
Essential Concepts
00695190 Book/CD Pack $17.95

Harmonics for Guitar
by Jamie Findlay
Private Lessons
00695169 Book/CD Pack $9.95

Jazz Guitar Chord System
by Scott Henderson
Private Lessons
00695291 . . . . $6.95

Jazz Guitar Improvisation
by Sid Jacobs
Master Class
00695128 Book/CD Pack $17.95

Modern Approach to Jazz, Rock & Fusion Guitar
by Jean Marc Belkadi
Private Lessons
00695143 Book/CD Pack $12.95

Music Reading for Guitar
by David Oakes
Essential Concepts
00695192 . . . . $16.95

Rhythm Guitar
by Bruce Buckingham & Eric Paschal
Essential Concepts
00695188 . . . . $16.95

Rock Lead Basics
by Nick Nolan & Danny Gill
Master Class
00695144 Book/CD Pack $14.95

Rock Lead Performance
by Nick Nolan & Danny Gill
Master Class
00695278 Book/CD Pack $16.95

Rock Lead Techniques
by Nick Nolan & Danny Gill
Master Class
00695146 Book/CD Pack $14.95

BASS

Arpeggios for Bass
by Dave Keif
Private Lessons
00695133 . . . . $12.95

Bass Fretboard Basics
by Paul Farnen
Essential Concepts
00695201 . . . . $12.95

Bass Playing Techniques
by Alexis Sklarevski
Essential Concepts
00695207 . . . . $14.95

Grooves for Electric Bass
by David Keif
Private Lessons
00695265 Book/CD Pack $12.95

Music Reading for Bass
by Wendy Wrehovcsik
Essential Concepts
00695203 . . . . $9.95

Odd-Meter Bassics
by Dino Monoxelos
Private Lessons
00695170 Book/CD Pack $14.95

KEYBOARD

Music Reading for Keyboard
by Larry Steelman
Essential Concepts
00695205 . . . . $12.95

R & B Soul Keyboard
by Henry J. Brewer
Private Lessons
00695327 . . . . $16.95

Salsa Hanon
by Peter Deneff
Private Lessons
00695226 . . . . $10.95

DRUM

Brazilian Coordination for Drumset
by Maria Martinez
Master Class
00695284 Book/CD Pack $14.95

Chart Reading Workbook for Drummers
by Bobby Gabriele
Private Lessons
00695129 Book/CD Pack $14.95

Working the Inner Clock for Drumset
by Phil Maturano
Private Lessons
00695127 Book/CD Pack $16.95

VOICE

Sightsinging
by Mike Campbell
Essential Concepts
00695195 . . . . $16.95

ALL INSTRUMENTS

An Approach to Jazz Improvisation
by Dave Pozzi
Private Lessons
00695135 Book/CD Pack $17.95

Encyclopedia of Reading Rhythms
by Gary Hess
Private Lessons
00695145 . . . . $19.95

Going Pro
by Kenny Kerner
Private Lessons
00695322 . . . . $19.95

Harmony & Theory
by Keith Wyatt & Carl Schroeder
Essential Concepts
00695161 . . . . $17.95

Lead Sheet Bible
by Robin Randall
Private Lessons
00695130 Book/CD Pack $19.95

WORKSHOP SERIES

Transcribed scores of the greatest songs ever!

Blues Workshop
00695137 . . . . $19.95

Classic Rock Workshop
00695136 . . . . $19.95

R & B Workshop
00695138 . . . . $19.95